D1133276

CONAN

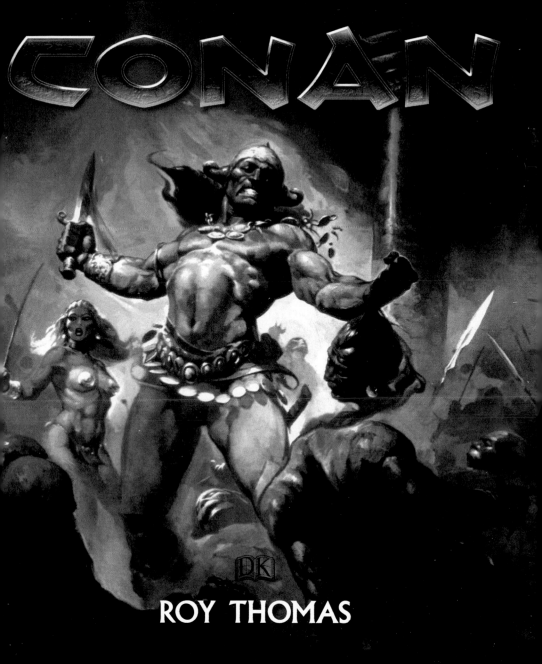

ROY THOMAS

LONDON, NEW YORK, MELBOURNE,
MUNICH, DELHI

Editor Brian Saliba
Senior Designer Mark Johnson Davies
Art Director Dirk Kaufman
Managing Art Editor Michelle Baxter
Production Manager Ivor Parker
Executive Managing Editor Sharon Lucas
Publishing Director Carl Raymond
DTP Coordinator Kathy Farias
Design Assistant Bill Miller

This American Edition 2007
First published in the United States by
DK Publishing
375 Hudson Street
New York, New York 10014

06 07 08 09 10 9 8 7 6 5 4 3 2 1
CD165 - 08/06

Page Design and Layout
Copyright © 2006 DK Publishing.

CONTENTS

CONAN

IN THE NEMEDIAN CHRONICLES

Know, O prince, that between the years when the oceans drank Atlantis and the gleaming cities, and the years of the rise of the Sons of Aryas, there was an Age undreamed of, when shining kingdoms lay spread across the world like blue mantles under the stars—Nemedia, Ophir, Brythunia, Hyperborea, Zamora with its dark-haired women and towers of spider-haunted mystery, Zingara with its chivalry, Koth that bordered on the pastoral lands of Shem, Stygia with its shadow-guarded tombs, Hyrkania whose riders wore steel and silk and gold. But the proudest kingdom of the world was Aquilonia, reigning supreme in the dreaming west. Hither came Conan, the Cimmerian, black-haired, sullen-eyed, sword in hand, a thief, a reaver, a slayer, with gigantic melancholies and gigantic mirth, to tread the jeweled thrones of the Earth under his sandaled feet."

So reads the sole surviving fragment of the fabled Nemedian Chronicles from the dim and distant Hyborian Age. Little is known of these Chronicles, save that they were written down by scribes in Nemedia, the second-mightiest kingdom in the west of that long-ago day, and that they recorded—among perhaps other things—the life and legends associated with the matchless Cimmerian soldier of fortune known as Conan the Barbarian....

FACTS—OR FANTASY?

The few undisputed facts concerning Conan's life are all contained in 21 stories of varying lengths, plus a handful of uncompleted tales and lean outlines, which were written between 1932 and 1936 by Robert E. Howard of Cross Plains, Texas.

It's not known how this young writer for American pulp magazines learned so much about the life and times of a warrior who lived and fought many millennia ago. But perhaps some hint may be gleaned from letters he wrote to fellow authors about how Conan "seemed to step full-grown into my consciousness when I wrote the first yarn of the series." He said it was as if, for weeks at a time, the Cimmerian "took complete possession of my mind and crowded out everything else"—as if Conan were standing at his shoulder, telling aloud stories that Bob merely transcribed.

The barbarian did not relate his exploits in the order they had happened to him. As Bob Howard explained: "The average adventurer, telling tales of a wild life at random, seldom follows any ordered plan, but narrates episodes widely separated by space and years, as they occur to him." It has been left to later scriveners to arrange these occurrences in roughly chronological order.

HERE BE LEGENDS

Besides this authentic canon, the subsequent years have given rise to an unverifiable but often fascinating body of lore around the larger-than-life figure of Conan. Such tales may or may not be based on actual events that occurred in that distant eon. We have tried, in these pages, to make it clear when we are dealing with episodes or entities whose truth is not vouched for by the writings of Robert E. Howard himself.

Perhaps some or all of these things actually did happen. Perhaps none of them did. Yet they are all part of the illustrious legend of Conan.

Let us begin to explore the exciting and eldritch world of this savage, sword-wielding Cimmerian...

...A THIEF... A REAVER...
A SLAYER...

THE HYBORIAN AGE

Conan lived during the era that scholars and dreamers alike call "The Hyborian Age." But mankind's lost prehistory extends back much farther even than that.

The Nemedian Chronicler referred to that earlier period as "The Pre-Cataclysmic Age," which probably occurred 15 to 20 millennia ago. This era gave rise to the Thurian civilization, the waning days of which were dominated by the mainland kingdoms of Valusia, Grondar, Thule, and others, all of whom spoke a common language. But that time had its barbarians as well, including the Picts, the Atlanteans, and the Lemurians. These tribes dwelt on islands or small continents far out on the Western Ocean. The Atlanteans were the ancestors of the Cimmerians—the race from which Conan

would one day spring—and the mightiest of them all was Kull of Atlantis, who rose to become king of civilized Valusia.

"Then," as Robert E. Howard wrote, "the Cataclysm rocked the world."

BARBARIANS IN A STRANGE NEW WORLD

The Great Cataclysm! Volcanoes and earthquakes destroyed the mighty Thurian cities, reducing their once-proud culture to savagery. Atlantis and Lemuria sank beneath the seas, and the Pictish Isles were heaved up, forming the mountain peaks of a new continent.

In the centuries that followed, the untamed island races migrated to the mainland in seagoing vessels, where the Atlanteans and the Picts fought a series of bloody wars that left both sides in a near-bestial state. The Lemurians were enslaved for thousands of years by an ancient race on the main continent, and theirs became a history of brutal servitude.

THE RISE OF THE HYBORIANS

The first tribe of survivors to begin the steep climb back to a state of civilization were the Hybori, for whom this age is named. This was a time of wanderings and conquests, as tribes mingled and mixed and formed new peoples. The first of the Hyborian realms to come into existence was Hyperborea, whose inhabitants turned abruptly from a nomadic life and began erecting dwellings of naked stone in the far north.

In the years that followed, other Hyborians founded kingdoms of their own. The first of these was the more southerly state of Koth, which bordered the lands of the nomadic clans that would soon establish the domain called Shem. The dusky-skinned Zhemri, who were descended from the remnants of one of the Thurian nation-states, founded the eastern kingdom of Zamora. And a hybrid race, formed of Picts, Hyborians, and the agrarian dwellers of the Valley of Zingg, brought forth a kingdom all their own. They called it Zingara.

They ruled a territory to the south of the great River Styx, which wound its way like a serpent to the Western Ocean. Other branches of once-Lemurians trekked eastward, where they gradually evolved into the Hyrkanians and the Khitans. And all the while, the dark-skinned tribal inhabitants of the far south lived in isolation.

This, then, was the high Hyborian Age.

This was the Age of Conan.

THE AGE OF CONAN

Over the next 4,000 or 5,000 years, many of the migrating clans gradually built new and civilized nation-states in the large central land mass, including Aquilonia, Nemedia, Ophir, Brythunia, Argos, Corinthia, and the Border Kingdom. The Picts, however, remained in a state of unbridled savagery.

Meanwhile, dwelling north of Aquilonia were the Cimmerians, ferocious Atlantean-descended barbarians untamed by any invaders. Still farther north, other strands developed into the red-haired inhabitants of Vanaheim and the blond denizens of Asgard.

The descendants of the Lemurians at last rebelled, threw off their masters' yoke, and became the Stygians.

"... there was an age undreamed of..."

NORDHEIM

VANAHEIM

ASGARD

HYPERBO

SNOW
DEVIL
GLACIER

Haloga

Pohiola

Sigtona

HYPERBOREA

SKULL GATE OF

CIMMERIA

Mount Crom

the
NORTHL

Field of the
Chiefs

Korvela

PICTISH WILDERNESS

Venarium

Aluz's Fortress

GRAASKAL MTS

BRYTHUNIA

Mount Golamira

BORDER KINGDOM

NEMEDIA

Izud

Yaralet

AQUILONIA

Galparan

Tanasul

Belverus

Numalia

CORINTHIA

ZAMORA

Shadizar

Tarantia

Shamar

Ianthe

OPHIR

Polopponi

Daramish

KHAURAN

KINGS

Zam

Sha

Akhlat

ZINGARA

Korda va

Khorshemish

KOTH

KOTHIAN DESERT

KHORAJA

Eruk

SHAN & SORB
The Red Waste

EAST

DES

ARGOS

Messantia

Asgalun

SHEM

Shushan

Kuthchemes

Troll Isles

Barachan
Isles

Isle of the
Black Ones

Isle of
Siptah

Khemi

RIVER STYX

Luxur

Set

STYGIA

Ptesion

haunted
Pyramid

MAP OF THE
HYBORIAN
WORLD

THIS MAP OF THE KNOWN WORLD AT THE TIME OF
CONAN THE CIMMERIAN IS BASED ON A CHART
DRAWN BY ROBERT E. HOWARD.

Sukhmet

KUSH

Xuthal

DARFAR

Xuchotl

Gazal

Tombalku

KESHAN

Alkmeenon

Keshia

PUNT

DRUJISTAN
Yanaidar

Kassali

IRANIS

Nameless Isle

BLACK

Kulalo

KINGDOMS

ZEMBABWEI

The Forbidden City
Old Zimbabwei

0	300	600	1200

Scale in Miles

Abombi

Isles of the South

Zanyoga

Sythia

LOULAN PLATEAU

PATHENIA

KARA KORUM
desert of Black Sand

Wan Tengri

HYRKANIA

Isle of Iron Statues

Rhamdam

ZAREHAANA

STEPPES

VILAYET

SEA

Onagrul

KUSAN

Khoraf

GREAT WALL OF KHITAI

KHITAI

Wuhuan Desert

Seeunderam

Khawarism

Swamps of the Dead

Shu Chen

LEMURIA

Shaulun

Psikang

Ruo Gen

EASTERN OCEAN

MOUNTAINS OF NIGHT

Xapur the Fortified

Kolchian

himelian
Mount
Yimsha
AFGHULISTAN

MERU

GHULISTAN

Numoi
Ayodhya
Gwandiakan
Forest of Ghendai

NJRUR

KOSALA

Peshkhauri

KAMBUJA

ANGKHOR

Khorala

Yota-Pong

VENDHYA

EQUATOR

Isles of Pearl

Misty Isles

MU

SOUTHERN SEA

MAJOR GODS OF THE HYBORIAN AGE

CROM

Like most lands of the Hyborian Age, Cimmeria had many gods, and at one time or another Conan swore by all of them! Their names were Lir, Mannanan, Morrigan, Badb, Macha, Nemain, and Crom.

Although not given to theological discussion, Conan did at times make known his feelings on the afterlife: "There is no hope here or hereafter in the cult of my people. In this world men struggle and suffer vainly, finding pleasure only in the bright madness of battle; dying, their souls enter a gray, misty realm of clouds and icy winds, to wander cheerlessly throughout eternity."

CONAN ON CROM

We know little about Crom, except what Conan said about him: "Their chief is Crom. He dwells on a great mountain. What use to call on him? Little he cares if men live or die. Better to be silent than to call his attention to you; he will send you dooms, not fortune! He is grim and loveless, but at birth he breathes power to strive and slay into a man's soul. What else shall men ask of the gods?"

When his pirate mate Belit asked him if he feared the gods, he replied, "I would not tread on their shadow." Which we should take as a "yes."

CROM DESCENDS?

According to one tale, Crom did intervene directly in the affairs of Conan once, and once only. While attempting to rescue his wife Zenobia from a Khitan wizard, Conan was attacked by demons. While teetering on the brink of death, he saw a great and gloomy hall. On a throne surrounded by somber warriors sat the tall, moody, black-maned, dark-eyed god himself, and he was not about to allow the "black arts of the East" to have Conan's soul. A great light flared from the god's outstretched hand, renewing the barbarian's ebbing strength.

HALL OF A GOD
One legend states that Conan was once granted a vision of Crom in a hall built of giant logs, but most agree that Crom dwelt deep in a mountain.

YMIR

He was the frost-giant, the principal godling of Vanaheim and Asgard. He ruled over Valhalla, the legendary hall where the souls of dead warriors congregated. It is possible that some of these warriors were reincarnated as lesser frost-giants, such as the hapless pair that once tried to stand between Conan and a woman he was pursuing. That woman, of course, was Ymir's daughter Atali. Like the Valkyries of later Norse myth, she was known to appear to those who had been mortally wounded in battle.

While we know little of Ymir's cult or rites, he seems to have been primarily a god of storm and of battle. It is likely that blood sacrifices were made to him—sacrifices that may or may not have included human beings.

RITES... AND WRONGS?
Ymir was a god of battle, and some scholars believe that the blood lust of his followers often led them to make grisly sacrifices in his name.

OLD WARRIORS DON'T DIE... THEY GO TO VALHALLA
At times Valhalla was described as a domain of snow-covered plain and at others as a vast hall.

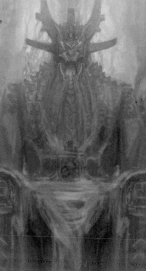

MITRA

He was a civilized person's god, whose followers believed him to be omnipresent. No human being could ever know what Mitra actually looked like, but he was often depicted "in idealized human form, as near perfection as the human mind can achieve." One statue of him in the eastern desert kingdom of Khoraja was known to speak to those who came before it, although some suspected that it was actually a priest of Mitra doing the talking from behind an ornate screen or curtain.

THIS I BELIEVE...

Mitra did not require even animal sacrifice, let alone the ritual slaughter of human beings that was all too common in the Hyborian Age. In Mitraic theology, there was a heaven and a hell, and men's souls were subject to judgement, based upon the kind of lives they led. Some even believed that Mitra wanted people to forgive their enemies, in a foreshadowing of the "golden rule" of a much later era.

Mitra's votaries seem to have tolerated the worship of other gods—as long as Mitra was acknowledged as supreme. And there seem to have been saints in the Mitraic universe, as men were heard to swear by them on occasion.

If there existed a female consort for Mitra, her name is no longer known. As one scholar phrased it: "Mitra stood essentially alone."

THE FACE OF GOD
One carved statue of Mitra had the aspect of a handsome man with magnificent shoulders, a patriarchal beard, and thick curls of hair confined by a simple band about the temples.

ON YOUR FEET
Mitraic temples were civilized places, where worshippers were expected to stand upright before their god, not crawl about on their bellies like worms.

ISHTAR

To many, the chief god was a woman, Ishtar. The practice of worshipping this goddess originated with the nomadic Sons of Shem, the people who would eventually found a kingdom of that name.

Ishtar was known as the Earth-Mother, and if there were any male gods in the pantheon of the Shemites, their names are unknown to us—so completely did goddess-worship eclipse all other rituals in that pastoral land.

THE LONG AND INVITING ARMS OF THE GODDESS

Although a Shemitish goddess in origin, during Conan's time Ishtar was also worshipped in the Hyborian land of Koth, as well as a few smaller kingdoms that had been founded by

THE ONE AND ONLY
Ancillary incarnations of Ishtar were known as Ashtoreth and Derketo, but neither were as revered as the great Earth-Mother herself.

Kothians. This was probably because Koth's king held sway over much of Shem, and there was a great deal of intermarriage, trade, and other contact between the two peoples. And so, even in Koth, the worship of Ishtar gained precedence over that of Mitra.

A TASTE OF THE EXOTIC

Ishtar's temples were rich, lavish, and exotic. They must have held great appeal to westerners who found Mitra too dry, too distant, too cerebral.

Her colorful rituals included ornate ceremony and blood sacrifice—although only of animals. According to one scholar, "her ivory idols combined southern sensuousness with northern restraint."

Major Gods of the Hyborian Age

THE FATE OF THE INFIDEL
Set was a god of darkness, and nonbelievers were often subjected to unspeakable rites and dooms far worse than death.

SET This was the major god of Stygia, that mysterious land of pyramids and serpents south of the River Styx. His image—his totem—was the serpent. Indeed, pythons that dwarfed any seen in our modern world lay coiled within his sinister subterranean temples. These reptiles were known to slither forth by night to devour hapless folk who walked the streets of Stygian cities—and, because the snakes were held sacred, no man dared raise a hand to stop them.

In the days of the evil empire of Acheron, some 3,000 years before Conan lived, much of the world was dominated by Set, who then was worshipped in both Acheron and Stygia. By Conan's time, however, worship of Set was confined to Stygia and the regions under that nation's influence. The Hyborians to the north did not consider Set to be a god at all, but merely an arch-demon!

BEHIND CLOSED TEMPLE DOORS

Little is known of the rituals of Set's religion, since Stygians hated foreigners. But Conan himself encountered sinister processions of masked priests in the streets of Khemi, the Stygian capital, and wholesale human sacrifices were not unheard of. It was a point of faith among the priesthood of Set that "blood aids great sorcery."

THE BLACK RING

Although many priests of Set were known to be mages, the most feared of these were those whom the Chronicler of the Conan tales called "the grisly wizards of the Black Ring... grim votaries who practice their abominable sorceries amid the black vaults of Stygia and the knighted domes of accursed Sabatea." This was an inner circle composed of the most powerful followers of Set. Chief among these in Conan's time was Thoth-amon, although the resurrected Xaltotun could have given him a challenge for primacy had he survived his encounter with the Cimmerian.

TARIM Like Erlik, Tarim was a principal god of the Turanians and their ancestral people, the Hyrkanians. Although less sinister than Erlik, Tarim's origins and nature are likewise obscure and half-forgotten. By most accounts, he is a deity to be sworn by, and nothing more.

THE WAR OF THE TARIM

Still, in one epic cycle known as "The War of the Tarim," he was a very real presence on Earth, for a time. That tale relates how Tarim was thought to be a man, the reincarnation of a being who had founded the Hyrkanian race in the days before the Cataclysm. Hyrkanians from the city-state of Makkalet kidnapped this man-god from his temple in Turan, prompting Prince Yezdigerd himself to lead a seaborne assault on Makkalet, destroying the city and reclaiming its god.

Conan, however, had seen the truth: the "Living Tarim" was in truth nothing more than a mentally defective man, who was incinerated

in a temple fire as the city fell. Yet even his corpse was treated as a holy relic. What real events or lotus dreams may lie behind the saga of the War of the Tarim is for scholars to debate.

BEHOLD YOUR GOD!
The death of the supposed man-god Tarim did not prevent Yezdigerd from parading its burnt skeleton through the streets in his hour of glory before returning it to Aghrapur.

AND, AT THE FOREFRONT OF IT ALL, THREE MAGNIFICENT FIGURES WHICH CAUSE BOTH SOLDIERY AND CAMP-FOLLOWERS TO GASP WITH FAWNING AWE..!

ERLIK

He was one of the chief gods of Turan, the eastern empire that grew in strength and rapaciousness during the Hyborian Age. But despite the fact that he was worshipped by the lordly classes in Aghrapur and the other great Turanian cities, virtually nothing is known of him or of his cult.

One scholar of things Hyborian identifies the Erlik worshipped in Conan's day with a legendary entity of the same name who was also called "The Lord of the Black Throne." Like Lucifer in the poetry of our era's John Milton, this Erlik rebelled against the creator god. For his impudence he was cast into darkness. But, by way of compensation, he became thereafter, in that scholar's words, "the ruler of seven demon-haunted underworlds, from which his emissaries went out nightly to hunt down the souls of evil-doers and recruit them for his black forces."

A SIGN OF DEVOTION
Like Set, Erlik was a dark god. His worshippers were known to perform violent acts on his behalf, and some of them even filed their teeth to sharp points... the better to draw out the sacrificial blood from nonbelievers.

ASURA

Vendhya, far to the east of the Hyborian kingdoms and even of Turan, was home to the god Asura. As one would expect when dealing with civilizations more than 120 centuries in the past, little has been recorded concerning the ceremonies of this cult. However, it is known that they believed in a heaven and a hell, the judgment of souls after death, and the promise of purification and forgiveness of sins.

ASURANS ABROAD
Unlike the sinister and hated Stygians, Vendhyans established worship centers in other lands, including Aquilonia. But because the Asurans' rituals were a secret and the very location of their temples often were unknown to the local populace, they were wrongly believed by many Aquilonians to be cannibals who prayed to the Stygian god Set. This belief was apparently bolstered by the Asurans' excessive clannishness and their customary black garb.

FRIENDS IN STRANGE PLACES
In a surprising turn of events, the fugitive King Conan once found succor in the temple of Asura at Tarantia. When he reclaimed his throne, he repaid the sect by lifting its outcast status in Aquilonia.

FOR, THEIR DEVIOUS ROUTE HAS CONFUSED EVEN *HIS* PRIMITIVE SENSE OF DIRECTION.

GREETINGS, MAJESTY...

WHERE ARE WE?

SPEAK UP, WHOEVER YOU ARE!

THIS IS NO BULL
The god Pteor, according to some scribes, was often depicted in the form of a bull—but clearly not always, as in this rendering from a legend of the Hyborian Age.

PTEOR

This god was one of the chief deities of Pelishtia, a Shemitish nation, but we know practically nothing of him or of his worship. Some 2,000 years or more after the Great Cataclysm, the Hyborian meadowlands were invaded from the east by clans of nomadic savages known as "the Sons of Shem." Having conquered that land, the interlopers combined with the agricultural locals to form the land called Shem.

Their religions—like their blood—became intermingled. The deity of each nomadic tribe was a sky-god, who was thought to command the weather. This male god was also thought to have mated with the Earth-Mother of the original inhabitants.

One scholar suggests that "Pteor probably evolved along these lines." However, this does not explain why the god was often depicted as an obscenely obese creature by some of his followers, or why others would claim that his true form was that of a bull.

ON A GRANITE THRONE SITS THE MONSTROUS AND OBSCENE PTEOR, THE GOD OF THE PELISHTIM...

...HIS EXAGGERATED ATTRIBUTES REFLECTING THE GROSSNESS OF HIS CULT, IN HIS LAP A LIMP WHITE FIGURE

THE BLOOD DEFILERS

Adventurers traveling through the uncharted wilds of Hyboria occasionally reported dreadful encounters with these remnants of the dark kingdom of Acheron—though doubtless many more never lived to tell the tale. Born of macabre sacrificial rituals and composed of congealed blood surrounding a magical stone heart, they were said to be the guardians of six sacred statues that dripped blood into basins below. If a traveler wished to treat with these devils, he had to offer a blood sacrifice of his own.

CONAN

THE CIMMERIAN

Conan was born into a clan that claimed an area in the north-western part of hill-capped Cimmeria. His grandfather was a member of a southern Cimmerian tribe who fled from his own people because of a blood feud. After long wanderings, which included journeys to the Hyborian lands to the south, he returned to Cimmeria and took refuge with another tribe in the north. At night before a roaring fire, he would spin elaborate tales of his travels—and no eyes would have grown wider at each telling than the fierce blue orbs of his black-maned grandson.

BORN ON A BATTLEFIELD

Conan's mother's name is given in one source as Greshan, his father's as Corin—some even say he had a sister. However, nearly every detail concerning Conan's family and lineage is cloaked in mystery—even the name of his tribe, though it may have been "Snowhawk." We know that Conan himself was born during a pitched fight between his own tribe and a horde of raiding Vanir, as the inhabitants of Vanaheim were known, but nothing more of his life before the age of young manhood is established beyond dispute. It seems likely, however, that both Conan's parents were dead by the time he wandered south to pursue his destiny.

THE BOY IS FATHER TO THE MAN

From childhood, Conan seems to have been a hardy specimen and a fighter to be reckoned with. Before he had seen fifteen snows, his name was repeated around the council fires. One account says that while still a boy, he fought off an entire pack of wolves barehanded, saving the life of a hunter trapped beneath a fallen tree, and that he finally killed the lead wolf by tearing its throat out with his teeth.

Another relates how, at the age of fourteen, he made a name for himself in his tribe by slaying a fellow tribesman who tried to murder him. According to yet another legend, he was sent out into the wooded hills on his fifteenth birthday to undergo rites of survival, and while there, he was initiated into the ways of man and woman by a mysterious beauty called Ursula, who roamed the wilderness in the company of two great white bears.

Whatever the truth behind any of these exploits, it is not difficult to imagine Conan performing them all, and numerous others besides.

THE FROST-GIANT'S DAUGHTER

Wounded in combat with the Vanir called Heimdul, Conan collapsed in the snow somewhere in the borderland between Vanaheim and Asgard. Upon waking, he beheld a beautiful young woman wearing only a veil of thinnest gossamer against the bitter cold of the North. To him, she looked "like Dawn running naked on the snows." He asked her to lead him to her village, but she only laughed and ran away. And so he struggled to his feet and pursued her.

THE FROST-GIANTS

Were the towering, axe-wielding figures who barred Conan's way to the girl merely human warriors of gigantic stature? Or were they what they later seemed to him: frost-giants, those more-than-human denizens of

-- he did not think of it long.

the frozen wastes? Whatever they were, the fleeing beauty called them "brothers"—and Conan soon realized that with her laughter and taunts, she had deliberately led him to them. Standing before them, he knew at once that these behemoths meant to slay him.

But be they men or something more, they had never encountered anyone like the Cimmerian, whose terrible, swift sword slew them both. Their monstrous corpses at his feet, Conan continued his pursuit of the girl.

THE ATLANTEAN SWORD

According to one legend, Conan discovered in an abandoned crypt, "A broadsword... made of blued iron. It might have been one of the first iron weapons borne by the hand of man: the legends of Conan's people remembered the days when men hewed and thrust with ruddy bronze, and the fabrication of iron was unknown." The tale goes on to say: "Many battles had this sword seen in the dim past, for its broad blade, although still keen, was notched in a score of places where, clanging, it had met other blades of sword and ax in the slash and parry of the melee... it was still a weapon to be feared."

A VISION IN WHITE
Conan knew not whether to trust his senses when the beautiful girl appeared to him. But as he pursued her, it was clear that his desire was for more than food and shelter.

SO NEAR... AND YET...

Whatever else she was, the girl was flesh and blood—and Conan meant to have her. But she broke away from his embrace, leaving her frail garment in his hand. Sprawling at last in the snow, she flung her arms up to the glowing Northern Lights and cried: Ymir! O my father, save me!" The next moment, the sky crackled with icy fire, and she vanished in a blinding blue flame. Conan heard nothing but rolling thunder, a sound like that of "a gigantic war chariot, rushing behind steeds whose frantic hoofs struck lightning from the snows and echoes from the skies."

YMIR'S OFFSPRING

Niord and his Aesir came upon Conan, unconscious in the snow, and revived him. Gorm, the oldest said that once, when sorely wounded as a youth, he had seen the very girl Conan described. She was Atali, daughter of the god Ymir the frost-giant, and she derived perverse pleasure from showing herself to the dying. The others scoffed—until they saw in Conan's fist, "a wisp of gossamer that was never spun by human distaff."

THE FROST-GIANTS
From the Nemedian Chronicles: "The giants answered with roars like the grinding of icebergs on a frozen shore and heaved up their shining axes as the maddened Cimmerian hurled himself upon them."

CROM...

AFTER THE BATTLE

"The clangor of the swords had died away, the shouting of the slaughter was hushed; silence lay on the red-stained snow." Conan was alone, but not for long...

THE MISTS OF TIME

Did Conan's encounter with Atali occur during his extreme youth, when he first adventured with the Aesir, who ranged far afield, battling Vanir and Hyperboreans alike? Or did it occur a few years later, when he had returned north briefly after his wanderings amid the civilized nations? Some have argued for the latter, since the account in the Nemedian Chronicles refers to "the palm and rose gardens of Poitain," which a very young Conan could not have seen. But it is the Chronicler, not Conan, who refers to that southern province of Aquilonia; thus, most scholars today number it among the young barbarian's earliest exploits.

This episode of Conan's life, alone of all recorded by Robert E. Howard himself, cannot be firmly placed in relation to others. But perhaps that is only fitting. For, surely, memories can be as fleeting as a tantalizing glimpse of the frost-giant's daughter.

THE THING IN THE CRYPT

According to one legend, Conan, having been imprisoned in Hyperborea, managed to strangle his jailer and made a break southward. Taking refuge from wolves in an abandoned crypt, he lit a fire, which revealed a huge, nigh-skeletal humanoid figure seated upon a throne made of stone, a horned helmet on his skull, a naked sword across his knees. The sight nearly scared the 16-year-old Conan out of his superstitious wits! The Cimmerian had sore need of a weapon, but when he overcame his fear of the supernatural enough to heft the blade, the hulking cadaver rose and lumbered horrifically toward him. Even its own sword would not hurt this undead Thing. Only with fire did Conan manage to destroy the creature. Then, new sword in hand, he emerged into the night and "once more set his footsteps to southward."

CONAN

THE THIEF

To survive in the civilized lands, a young barbarian needed employment. But when Conan wandered south for the first time, he had no certain way of earning his daily bread—let alone a flagon of wine. Given his skill with a blade, some have asked why he didn't at once become a mercenary soldier—a "sellsword." And perhaps he would have done so, had the opportunity presented itself. On the other hand, he was brought up in a land where nothing short of an Aquilonian invasion could unite the tribes even briefly, so it is hard to picture Conan submitting to even a hint of military discipline at age 16 or 17. Perhaps the life of a thief was an inevitability, after all.

LARCENY IN THE HYBORIAN AGE

Every city, even the tiniest hamlet, had its thieves—whether light-fingered pickpockets, swift-handed cutpurses, or armed robbers who depended as much on brute strength as on skill and stealth. But for most, the tools of the trade were as old as the profession. Pickpockets, if they didn't rely solely on lightness of touch (and fast legs to flee on), often wore arm slings to make potential victims believe they had an injured arm. "Cutpurses" did precisely that—using a very small (but very sharp!) knife held between their fingers. Far better to slice a hole in the side of a wealthy man's moneybag than to go rifling about it in, among coins that might jingle and jangle noisily. For climbing walls, grappling hooks were used.

Naturally, the more advanced thieves knew how to pick a lock—or at least how to cut through one with file and hacksaw. Either way, they would certainly have had to work as quickly as possible, while keeping an eye out for the nightwatch or a rich man's personal guardians, who, in the Hyborian Age, might not always have been human—or, strictly speaking, animal either.

A THIEF FROM CIMMERIA

Acccording to scholars who have studied his career, Conan was, in his youth "more daring than adroit." Ironic, considering that some of his first thefts occurred in Zamora, a kingdom famous for the quality of its thievery. Small wonder, too, that it took the lad some time to earn a reputation among the older, more skillful worshippers of Bel, the Shemitish god of thieves.

In addition to his known exploits in Zamora's City of Thieves, certain legends tell of his other early attempts to transfer the wealth of others to his own pockets. It's said that he once relieved tax money from the vaults of a wizard called Zukala, then neglected to return it to the villagers, as promised. (A good decision, once the treacherous townsmen were planning to slay him when he brought back their money!)

This same source says that a young woman of easy virtue once persuaded Conan to have a sackful of ill-gotten gold recast into the shape of a heart. She then stole it from him while he slept—even though he had just saved her from an enormous bat. Some cynics, however, claim this tale is merely a parable, yet another literary depiction of the "the prostitute with a heart of gold."

Another legend states that Conan and a Gunderman comrade once looted a long-lost city, but were set upon by armored skeletons. And what few coins Conan managed to spirit away soon turned into venomous serpents inside his moneybags!

NEVER STEAL FROM A MAN OF GOD(S)

Conan and the Gunderman reunited in one city-state or another—it may have been in Corinthia—and, working together, they enjoyed a small degree of success, for a time. But then they made the fatal mistake of stealing from a fat priest of the god Anu. The full-fed man of the cloth was well known for being a fence for stolen articles and a spy for the local police: "He worked a thriving trade both ways, because the district on which he bordered was the Maze, a tangle of muddy, winding alleys and sordid dens, frequented by the boldest thieves in the kingdom."

For one reason or another, the priest betrayed the Gunderman to the police, and he was hanged in the market square. Even as a thief, the Cimmerian youth clung to his own barbarian code of honor, so he evened the score by stealing into the temple of Anu and beheading the cleric. Having matured a bit, Conan knew that friendship bore certain responsibilities—and that among those was vengeance for a comrade's life.

By the time he was 19, he'd moved beyond the thieving phase of his life. He had come a long way since he left the forested hills of Cimmeria, but he still had much farther to go...

ON THE ROAD OF KINGS

The Road of Kings, often spoken of in tales of Conan, passed through many of the major Hyborian kingdoms. Though it is uncertain whether this important trade route began in Khauran or in Turan, it is known that it wound through Zamora, Corinthia, and Nemedia on its serpentine way westward, finally traversing Aquilonia and Argos to the Western Ocean. It is doubtful that these oft-warring nation-states ever managed to cooperate in anything so peaceful as road-building. More likely, the route was an ancient one, predating the Hyborian kingdoms. Regardless of its origin, the Road of Kings is probably the reason that young Conan made his way to Nemedia, rather than to some other locale.

NEMEDIA

Of all the Hyborian lands, only Aquilonia might lay claim to being more powerful than Nemedia. Separated by a high mountain range, the two kingdoms waged war on each other, off and on, for several centuries. Yet there was a tradition of scholarship in Nemedia, which is underscored by the existence of the famous Nemedian Chronicles. The greatest Nemedian cities were Belverus, the capital, and Numalia. Its king during Conan's younger years was named Nimed. That monarch was murdered and succeeded by his brother Tarascus, who then warred with King Conan of Aquilonia. Few kings of the Hyborian Age died with their crowns still firmly on their heads, and those of Nemedia were no exception.

CORINTHIA

At least half Corinthia's territory was composed of mountains. That rugged geography led to isolation and certainly contributed to its ability to remain unconquered by even the most powerful empires. We do know that like

Brythunia and the Border Kingdom in the North, Corinthia was a grouping of loosely allied city-states, but unfortunately, little other verifiable information has suvived.

ZAMORA

Bordered on the east by the Kezankian Mountains and by lesser ranges to the south and west, Zamora was founded several thousand years before Conan's time. Its capital was the aptly named Shadizar the Wicked, although equally

"...Zamora with its dark-haired women and towers of spider-haunted mystery..."

CITY OF SURPRISES
Although its actual name might have been Arenjun, to most it was known simply as the City of Thieves—the kind of place where a 150-foot tower might spring up overnight.

NUMALIA, THE "SECOND CITY"
It was in Numalia, the second-largest city of Nemedia, that Conan encountered the Man-Serpent in a house of antiquities.

well known was its City of Thieves, whose actual name is sometimes given as Arenjun. The local police dared not set foot in the notorious district called the Maul, "where the thieves of the East held carnival by night." There, cutpurses, kidnappers, and killers rubbed elbows and amused each other with ribald yarns of extralegal derring-do.

Most mysterious and sinister of all Zamora's municipalities was Yezud, the City of the Spider-God, where—if legends are to be believed—an arachnid the size of an elephant was worshipped as a deity. Conan is said to have slain the creature, whose name was variously given as Omm or Zath. One of its vile priests survived and gained the ability to transform himself at will into a leopard-sized arachnid.

SHADIZAR THE WICKED
Despite its intriguing epithet, little is known for certain about this Zamorian city. But if the legends are true, and young Conan ventured here, he no doubt came to relieve other men of excess wealth.

KEEP INVADERS OUT—KEEP SECRETS IN
Corinthia's extreme and mountainous terrain is likely the reason that the realm remained independent, even during the days of the empire of Acheron, some 3,000 years before Conan's day. It is also the reason we know so little about its people and customs.

CONAN

THE MERCENARY

During his various adventures as a starveling thief in Zamora and elsewhere, Conan gained his first tastes of professional fighting and Hyborian intrigue. And he found that he rather enjoyed them both. When he reached his early 20s, he decided it was time to find a new and more promising career. He would become a soldier of fortune or a mercenary soldier—a "sellsword," in the parlance of the times.

A SOLDIERLY SOJOURN IN TURAN

The exotic eastern kingdom of Turan was, at this time, in the process of acquiring an empire that would rival even Aquilonia and Nemedia. Such a goal required men to spearhead the banners, and according to several usually reliable sources, Conan served in the army of Turan for a spell. The circumstances under which he signed up, however, are murky, at best. One account says that while passing through Turan's capital of Aghrapur, he was given a choice: join King Yildiz's finest or be tossed into the royal dungeon. He chose the military life as the lesser of two evils.

WEAPONS OF WAR

Up to this point, Conan had depended on his own wits, along with his natural talent for swordplay and knife-wielding, to get him out of tight spots. But soldiering day by day with professional soldiers, some of whom had studied weaponry all their lives, soon convinced him he should broaden his basic skills. It is not known whether there was some particular master of blades who honed his inborn abilities, or whether he simply watched and learned.

Up to this point, he had scorned the bow and arrow as a weapon of cowards, the instrument of men who feared to come into close contact with an enemy. But he was impressed by the Hyrkanian horse archers, who formed an important branch of the Turanian cavalry and who could loose their arrows with great accuracy while thundering full-out on the back of a charging stallion. Soon Conan was a master of the bow, whether on foot or on horseback.

FAREWELL TO TURAN

Precisely when and why he resigned is unknown, but one account states that his desertion from Turan's military involved the wife of his cavalry commander. Be that as it may, Conan soon rode westward again, having heard that there were wars plenty in the offing back in the Hyborian lands.

SWORDS FOR SALE

After many adventures along the Road of Kings—no doubt including brief returns to thievery when the opportunity presented itself—Conan became a mercenary soldier under one of the many roving generals of that time.

It is even said that the commander of this group was none other than the nobleman Murilo, who had formed the Crimson Company—perhaps after his shady doings back home were finally discovered. This outfit sold its swords and services to the various city-states that were forever at war with each other. Whether under Murilo or another, Conan fared well during this interregnum, and learned ever more about the art of civilized warfare.

YOU CAN'T GO HOME AGAIN

During a lull in the wars, he returned for a short time to his native Cimmeria. In one tale that is told around certain campfires, he arrived to learn that a childhood playmate—now a lovely young woman—had been carried off by Vanir raiders. Although he was unable to save the doomed lass, he evened the score by dispatching a horde of the red-haired rogues in their own longhouse.

But suddenly such blood-raids and bouts of revenge seemed to him like a waste of his life. His love for adventure soon drew him southward once more... and, it would turn out, toward the first and perhaps the greatest love of his life.

ON THE SHORES OF THE INLAND SEA

In the long-forgotten Hyborian Age, when the great basin that would one day be the Mediterranean Sea was all flatlands and mountains, the greatest body of water between the Western Ocean and whatever vast body of water might lie beyond the distant East was the Vilayet Sea. On its eastern shores were the Hyrkanians, and on the western were their offshoots, the Turanians.

TURAN

The Turanians were descended from the Hyrkanians of an earlier eon, and they sometimes even referred to themselves as "Hyrkanians." In truth, they were the lords of their own great empire, which was destined to grow even greater in Conan's day. The kingdom boasted a large, powerful navy and several huge cities that ringed the western shore of the Sea. Skilled Turanian seamen aboard their famed war-galleys had made the Vilayet a "Turanian lake," in the vernacular of the day.

Turan's influence extended over most of the Hyrkanian heartland to the east, and its armies conquered many of the desert cities to the south, such as Zamboula, which had been established by Stygians. During Conan's lifetime, Turan was beginning to look westward, as well—casting dark, covetous eyes at the tempting farmlands and wealthy metropolises of Zamora, Shem, and the Hyborian kingdoms.

THE VILAYET SEA

The "Inland Sea," as it was often known in the Hyborian Age, was both a barrier to and a catalyst for the relations between its two major coastal nations, Hyrkania and Turan. The sea itself was perhaps 300 miles across at its widest point, and some 2,000 miles long. To any except

No Safe Harbor
Scattered with isles populated by savage peoples and carnivorous gray apes that dwarfed the gorillas of a later era, the Vilayet was no place for the faint-of-heart... a designation rarely applied to Conan the Cimmerian.

PATHENIA

"...Hyrkania whose riders wore steel and silk and gold."

H
Y
R
K
A
N
I
A

Rhamdam

ZAREHAANA

STEPPES

Onagrul

Khoraf

WUHUAN DESERT

Secunderam

ZAPOROSKA RIVER

MERU

MOUNTAINS

GHULISTAN

AFGHULISTAN

Jhumbda

Ayodhya

Gwandiakan

Forest of Ghendai

Peshkhauri

Khosa

OSALA

Wan Tengri

Lake Jhil

KUSAN

MOUNTAINS OF KHITAI

MOUNTAINS OF NIGHT

KOTA OTS

TALAKETARA KURU

KH

RIDERS OF RENOWN
From nomadic Hyrkanian tribes came the fabled mounted warriors and horse-archers that bolstered Turan's armies.

the great vessels of Turan, it might as well have been an endless ocean, dotted with mostly uninhabited islands. But those isles that were not without life were home to a wide range of horrors and inhuman entities of a bygone day.

HYRKANIA

The Hyrkanians were the descendants of the Lemurians, who fled to land when their chain of islands sank during the Great Cataclysm. Eventually freeing themselves from enslavement in far-eastern Khitai, they moved westward and gradually dominated the steppes on the eastern shore of the Vilayet Sea.

In Conan's day, Hyrkania was less a kingdom than a region in which isolated city-states held sway, separated from their neighbors by steppe, forest, desert, and even tundra. Although many of these city-states were dominated by the empire of Turan, others retained their autonomy, at least for at time—perhaps by trading with and paying tribute to the acquisitive kings in Aghrapur across the water. Some nomadic Hyrkanian tribes dwelt far from the sea and thus Turan's powerful navy. These often refused even to acknowledge Turan's existence.

CONAN

CORSAIR OF THE BLACK COAST

"I must go down to the sea again..." So wrote the English poet John Masefield... and Conan, twelve millennia earlier, would have understood. At several different points in his life, the Cimmerian became a seafarer—almost always outside the laws of nations. Call him pirate, buccaneer, or corsair, he often sailed in search of plunder and adventure.

SEA CHANGE

Conan was about twenty-four when the Road of Kings led him at last to Messantia, the major seaport of Argos. At the time, he had no intention of going to sea, but fate forced his hand. Hauled into court, he was ordered by an insolent judge to reveal the whereabouts of a comrade who had run afoul of the law. When he explained that he could not betray his friend, the judge threatened to toss him into a dungeon. At this point, Conan decided "they were all mad," and cleft the judge's skull with his sword. (And, while we may question allowing the barbarian to wear a sword into the courtroom, we should also consider what would have happened to anyone who tried to take it from him.)

Realizing he was now persona non grata in Messantia, Conan commandeered the nearest horse and galloped for the wharfs. There, he hopped aboard a merchant vessel just pulling away from the docks and at swordpoint ordered its captain, a man named Tito, not to turn back. Thus did Conan of landlocked Cimmeria go to sea for the first time aboard the *Argus*.

FIRST MEETING—FIRST MATE

Along the so-called Black Coast, the crew of the *Argus*, which now included the young barbarian, beheld the smoking ruins of villages and ebony corpses. One sunrise, they were attacked and boarded by the black corsairs from the *Tigress*, a pirate galley commanded by Bêlit, the self-styled "Queen of the Black Coast." Tito and all his crewmen died in the assault. Even Conan, shearing heads from shoulders while himself protected by armor, would have fallen to the sea of spears surrounding him—if the she-pirate herself had not intervened. On an impulse, she made the fierce Cimmerian her first mate—in more ways than one—and he entered a new phase of his ever-colorful life.

THE RAGE OF THE *TIGRESS*

For the next three years, Conan sailed with Bêlit as her ship ranged the seas, mostly between Stygia and the southernmost tip of the Black Coast. The villagers shuddered, aware that at any moment they might fall prey to pirates of their own race. Survivors of raided Stygian ships cursed both captain and first mate. But the Queen of the Black Coast and her barbarian mate were undaunted. As the Chronicles say, "Heedless as a vagrant wind, the *Tigress* cruised the southern coasts...."

ALL IS MYSTERY

The Black Coast was the name given to the lands that bordered on the Western Ocean south of priest-ridden Stygia. It was doubtless called that originally because of its fierce, dark-skinned inhabitants. But it earned its name twice over by remaining a region of which little was known, as if all light and knowledge were swallowed up as soon as one moved from those palm-lined shores into the somber vastness of the interior.

THE BLACK COAST

The earliest and most authentic maps of the Hyborian Age do not even list the names of the "nations" that comprised the Black Coast. Although it seems certain that the most northerly one was named Kush, the others were perhaps not truly kingdoms at all, but simply collections of isolated tribal lands. South of the Zarkheba River, all is mystery.

Even so, there is ample evidence suggesting that the tribes traded and communicated with each other, both on the Black Coast and further inland. During those few years that the white she-pirate Bêlit and her savage crew ranged those waters, drums beat out a voiceless warning to those further south that the she-devil buccaneer was headed their way. The villages trembled even before the sails of the dreaded *Tigress* hove into view, her decks swarming with warriors and bristling with spears.

After Bêlit's reign came to an end, the denizens of these southern climes were content to have little contact with each other or with northerners. And given their unfortunate experiences, who can blame them?

KUSH

The country called Kush, the capital of which has at times been given as "Meroë," was comprised mostly of villages along the shore of the Western Ocean. Plunging a few miles inland, careless travelers would have encountered first a band of almost impenetrable (although not uninhabited) rain forest, followed by a broad savanna, which was bordered on the east by hills.

Those in Kush who thought about things counted the Southern Desert, which lay beyond those hills, as part of their kingdom, but the supposed "kings" of the land exercised no control over the vast wasteland.

HAIL TO THE QUEEN
It is unknown whether Kush or other lands of the Black Coast ever had a true king. Perhaps that is one reason that the she-pirate Bêlit styled herself "Queen of the Black Coast."

KUSH... BUT ONLY IN NAME

Kush was the northernmost of the black kingdoms located to the south of Stygia. But because the Hyborians knew so little of the black lands, they often used the term "Kush" to refer to all of them indiscriminately. That would have included the countries of Darfar, Keshan, Punt, Zembawei, and perhaps others.

AMRA

During Conan's days of sailing the waters of the Black Coast with Bêlit, he gained the name "Amra," which means "the lion." Its origins are uncertain, although the Nemedian Chronicles do give us a hint: "Tom-toms beat in the night, with a tale that the she-devil of the sea had found a mate, an iron man whose wrath was as that of a wounded lion."

Less substantiated legends tell of an earlier "Amra." This crimson-haired jungle man was said to be the son of an Aquilonian nobleman. Having been raised among the great felines, he had become "Lord of the Lions" and had dared try to force himself upon Bêlit. Conan killed him in hand-to-hand combat.

Two decades later, Conan's deeds were still remembered by the people of the region, although few knew that the "Amra" of their legends was the same north-born barbarian who was then sitting upon the throne of Aquilonia.

LEGENDS OF AMRA AND BÊLIT

There exist few hard facts concerning Conan's sojourn with Bêlit, but many yarns have been spun. There are tales of tribesman of the interior riding the backs of great crocodiles known as "river-dragons," and of huge falcons being ridden by men of Harakht, the mythical "Hawk City" located somewhere on the River Styx. Ballads are sung of Kelka, the time-lost "city in the storm," and of an isle ruled by the Lord of the Feathered Serpent. It is even said that, at one point, Conan and Bêlit stormed King Ctesphon's palace, located in the Stygian capital at Luxur, and that they ran afoul of Thoth-amon's murderous Man-Serpents.

BEHIND THE LEGENDS

One thing verified by the Nemedian Chronicles is that it was during this period that Conan first encountered the scrawled symbol that he would come to know as the Sign of Jhebbal Sag. This powerful sigil could control the actions of wild beasts. Some say that one of Jhebbal Sag's votaries, Ajaga by name, crowned himself the "Beast King of the Black Coast" and, leading an army of animals from the jungle, briefly carved himself an empire.

It is also known that Bêlit occasionally traded with Argossean merchants, perhaps sneaking into Messantia by night to do so. Once, she, Conan, and the corsairs burned the "black walls" of Khemi, Stygia's major seaport—although it is unclear whether those "black walls" were the city's sea walls or its dark-prowed ships.

LION KING
Conan was known as Amra for the several years during which he ruled the Black Coast with Bêlit, who was, to put it mildly, rather taken with him from the very beginning.

TO THE VICTOR GO THE SPOILS
According to legend, after Conan killed the man known as Amra, he took over both his name and the great lion that had been the jungle king's own blood-brother.

CONAN

THE WARRIOR

The word "warrior" can have many meanings, and Conan was a warrior in many ways—and in many places—as he neared the age of 30. Penniless after his long trek north through the black kingdoms, where his reputation as Amra had stood him in good stead, he found himself again in need of gainful employment in the Hyborian lands. Thanks to the constant feuding between the greedy monarchs of Shem, Koth, and Ophir, there was always a market for a good sword-arm.

FABLES AND FOLLIES

Legends and fables of his exploits during this period are abundant, although some ring truer than others. He is said to have saved the throne for King Phehemenes, a Zingaran sovereign, and to have barely avoided becoming a casualty of the Zingaran Inquisition. It's even rumored that the barbarian briefly became a pirate along the coast of Vanaheim, although piracy so far north is not even hinted at in the Nemedian Chronicles. Still, who can say that a few of the most outrageous of these stories may not actually have happened?

KOTH AND KHORAJA

One frequent setting for many of these apocryphal stories is Koth, perhaps because it was one of the older Hyborian kingdoms and was large enough to touch both sea-girding Argos in the west, and the outer steppes of Turan in the east. In these tales, Koth seems to be the crossroads of the world and the place where

Conan is said to have encountered a number of incredible beings, including Imhotep, the Devourer of Souls. Two different legends from this time tell of Conan allying with a young prince from Khitai and briefly assuming the role of warlord for the Kothian city-state of El Shah Maddoc.

Conan's verifiable exploits during this time are exciting enough. It is known that he re-entered mercenary service in the western nations, rising to the position of captain under Amalric the Nemedian. In Khoraja, Conan was destined to become, for the first time, a true leader of men—an experience that perhaps set him on the road to becoming king of opulent Aquilonia.

SURVIVOR

In a prominent story cycle, Conan joined the army of King Sumuabi of Akkharia, a city-state in the south of Shem. Through treachery, Akkharia's forces were wiped out almost to a man and Conan was that man! Many scholars have questioned the Cimmerian's knack for being the sole survivor of so many conflicts. Explain it away as you will—as the vagaries of fate, or even as the Cimmerian god Crom looking after him, unlikely as that may seem—the most logical explanation is perhaps that Conan the barbarian was the greatest swordsman and fighter of his age.

That alone may suffice to explain why, at battle's end, when the smoke and dust cleared, he was often left standing alone, bloody blade in hand, amid a landscape bathed in carnage and destruction...

TRADE & WAR

ONE BRIEF SHINING MOMENT
Khoraja is seldom mentioned in the Nemedian Chronicles, but while Conan was general of its armies, deeds done there were widely celebrated.

THEN, AS THE HOST CAMPS FOR THE NIGHT FIERY-EYED KILLMEN DRIFT IN TO REPEAT RUMORS THAT HAVE COME OUT OF THE MYSTERIOUS DESERT.

SHEM

"The pastoral lands of Shem." Those words from the Nemedian Chronicles reveal what the rest of the known world thought of Shem during the Hyborian Age. Founded in ancient days by the nomads known as the Sons of Shem, its western regions were composed of fertile meadowlands, with cities lying at slightly higher elevations. Although the land became more arid as one traveled eastward, caravans never ceased crisscrossing the kingdom, and many cities fed off the traffic of trade going from west to east and from north to south. Asgalun and Anakia... Akkharia and Nippr... Shumir and Ghaza... all Shemite cities were crossroads at heart.

There were numerous wars between the cities of the meadows and the cities of the desert, between armies made up on both sides of grim horsemen with blue-black beards. The land gave birth to the Asshuria, a celebrated warrior-clan that is often mentioned in accounts of mercenary armies of that era.

Paradoxically, although trade flowed like a river through their country, the Shemites profited far more from the movement of goods than from trade of their own. Nor did they send ships to sea to transport goods either to or from their shores. As the Chronicles point out: "There was scant profit in trade with the fierce and wary sons of Shem." They were, for the most part, middlemen.

KHORAJA

Khoraja was the name of both the small kingdom nestled between Koth and the Eastern Desert and its principal city. In fact, that settlement was its *only* true city, for a map of the day reveals that no other towns within its mountainous borders were considered substantial enough to rate even a dot or a scribbled name.

As to its geography, Khoraja was separated from Shem by the formidable Kothian Escarpment, and its Shamla Pass was essential to caravans en route from the Hyborian lands to Turan or kingdoms to the south.

Once a part of Shem, Khoraja had been carved out of Shemite lands by the swords of Kothic adventurers many years before. And the people of Khoraja never lost their fervent desire for independence.

THEN, SHE HURRIES FORTH, BEFORE HER RESOLUTION MAY FALTER.

NEVER BEFORE HAS THIS DAUGHTER OF ARISTOCRATS VENTURED UNATTENDED OUTSIDE HER ANCESTRAL PALACE.

KHORAJAN NIGHTS
When Khoraja's young king was held captive by the ruler of Ophir, that pocket kingdom might easily have fallen... had the king's sister not paid heed to a prophesy that sent her out into the streets of the capital.

PRINCESS YASMELA

Yasmela never wanted to rule Khoraja. But when her brother, King Khossus, was held hostage by Ophir's sovereign, she had no choice. As fate would have it, the enigmatic leader known as "Natohk, the Veiled One" appeared during this time and united the desert nomads into a fanatical army bent on overrunning first Khoraja, then all the Hyborian lands.

A GOD MOVES IN MYSTERIOUS WAYS

After Natohk came to her in a nightmare vision, threatening both to conquer her kingdom and ravish her person, Yasmela prayed at the temple of Mitra for advice. Whether it was a god who spoke to her, or priests whispering from behind the altar, she heeded the advice: "Go forth upon the streets alone, and place your kingdom in the hands of the first man you meet there." That man turned out to be Conan, a soldier in Amalric's mercenary force.

TRIUMPH—AND A CELEBRATION

Yasmela rode with Conan as he led Khoraja's forces against the nomad horde—and scattered them. And when Natohk carried her off, Conan pursued them into ancient ruins. Before the Veiled One could sacrifice Yasmela to long-forgotten dark deities, the Cimmerian slew him. Then, the Nemedian Chronicles relate, "out on the desert, in the hills among the oceans of dead, men were dying, were howling with wounds and thirst and madness, and kingdoms were staggering," but this couldn't prevent Conan and Yasmela from making love on the

very altar upon which Thugra Khotan had meant to sacrifice her.

"MISTER QUEEN"

Conan's pride, however, refused to let him play "Mister Queen" to any woman, and soon he left Khoraja. By some accounts, not verified by the Chronicles, he rescued Yasmela's brother Khossus from a stronghold where he was held by men loyal to the King of Ophir. If true, Yasmela was probably only too happy to relinquish the throne upon his return.

A PRAYER FOR THE ANSWERING
Like all in Khoraja, Yasmela and her maidservant Vateesa had long since forsaken the worship of holy Mitra for that of the goddess Ishtar. But on this night, only the Lord of Light could save them...

A MOONLIT OFFER
When Conan realized who Yasmela was—and that her offer was as real as her need—he became commander of Khoraja's armies.

BRACING HERSELF, YASMELA STEPS FROM THE SHADOWS HER CLOAK HELD CLOSE ABOUT HER...

WHO THE DEVIL ?? AN AMBUSH!

A-COURTING WE WILL GO
It is said that Conan lingered for a time at the court of Yasmela—no doubt enjoying both the royal favor and the attendant scenery—before he moved on to other lands, other adventures.

CONAN
THE CHIEFTAN

Perhaps it all started the night that the sister to the captive king went out into the streets and put her kingdom's army into the hands of a stranger. When all was said and done, Conan had his first taste of leadership. But power is a cup from which a man, having lifted it once, will soon desire to drink again.

After the interlude in Khoraja, the Cimmerian, who had always been restless under the authority of other men, now sought the chance to lead whenever he encountered a new group. In the years that followed, more than one group of ruffians, brigands, and pirates approached Conan as if he were a victim, or at most a fellow cutthroat, only to find themselves happily following him into battle soon thereafter. On the steppes of Turan, it was the kozaki who paid homage to the barbarian shortly after crossing paths with him. And in the hills of Vendhya, the Afghuli hillmen followed suit.

In the case of the kozaks, he arrived in their midst all but empty-handed, but soon found that he had old friends among those fierce horsemen and the Red Brotherhood of the Vilayet Sea. When he united the groups under his command, the pickings were better than ever... for a time.

When his ultimate plan to weld the hill tribes into a single army failed, he simply shrugged and headed back whence he'd come. But, for better or worse, the tribes he'd led were changed forever.

RETURN TO THE EAST

TURAN

According to some tales, when Conan had first fought for Turan, it had been a kingdom. Now it had placed its booted foot on the path to empire, and it would no longer look the other way as kozaks and pirates nibbled away at its fringes.

VILAYET SEA

The Inland Sea, being finite, would seem to be an easy place for imperial forces to corner a foe. But the Vilayet was huge, and the ships of the Red Brotherhood had no trouble finding hiding places among its myriad isles and river inlets..

KHAURAN

Khauran lay between the eastern tip of Koth and the so-called Eastern Desert. Khauran, whose name was also given to its capital and principal city, was blessed with fertile soil and lush meadows. Like Khoraja, Khauran had been founded years before by Kothic adventurers in an era when such men carved several tiny kingdoms out of the eastern uplands. Politically, there seems to have been no tradition that demanded a king be the ruler, for Queen Taramis felt no pressure to wed.

THE EASTERN DESERT

The Eastern Desert itself had no firmly established boundaries. It was simply the name given to the whole great sandy

COOL WATER
More than once in his colorful life, Conan found himself wandering in one arid wasteland or another, although none more formidable than the Eastern Desert, where not even the oases were safe havens.

ROAD OF SAND
The Road of Kings trickled to a strand of golden sand when it reached the Eastern Desert, yet caravans were always found plying the barren wastes.

OLIVIA
She was a daughter of the king of Ophir, but when she refused to marry a prince of Koth, she was sold as a slave to a Shemite chief, who then gave her to Shah Amurath, lord of purple-gardened Akif. There, she endured his insatiable lust for some time, the memory of which stung her "like a slaver's whip." During a citywide celebration, she escaped from the him, but the brash warrior-lord overtook her. Only Conan's timely arrival saved her, after which Olivia had little choice but to accompany him to an uninhabited isle in the middle of the Vilayet Sea. When Conan emerged victorious over the horrors of that place, she was proud to share his life. And when their dalliance was over? Why, she was a survivor and the daughter of a king. Whatever the world threw at her next, she would be ready!

expanse that lay to the east of Stygia, and Shem, and the Hyborian lands. Beyond it to the east was Turan, whose borders were forever expanding westward.

VENDHYA

This ancient kingdom of the East was ruled by a royal family who were the scions of a warrior caste known as the Kshatriya. Its southwestern region was called Afghulistan, and to the north of Vendhya were the towering Himelian Mountains, whose more habitable areas were known as Ghulistan. The Nemedian Chronicles indicate that tropical Vendhya possessed rich agricultural lands, as well as many precious minerals, which made this sub-continent desirable to imperial Turan.

SWORDS AND SAND
The Eastern Desert was alive in more ways than one. There very wind was known to take the form of a loathsome sand demon, and not even the greatest swordsman of the age could slice burning, swirling sands with a blade.

OF VANISHED ISLES
Years before his days as a chieftan, Conan and his Vanir comrade Fafnir had sojourned briefly on the lost island of Bal-Sagoth, in the middle of the Vilayet Sea. But it had sunk beneath their very feet. When he returned nearly a decade later, he sailed over the exact spot.

CONAN

SOLDIER OF FORTUNE

In one sense, Conan was always a soldier of fortune, fighting for no cause but one he chose for himself. Not long after facing the terrors of the Black Seers of Yimsha, he left the hills of Vendhya for reasons unknown and hired out his blade to various employers, cutting a swath of legends along the way.

TALES AND TALONS

Tales abound in which the Cimmerian... accepted a commission from a village lord to rescue his daughter from a local warlord... led a gang of marauders against a rival gang led by a woman warrior known as Snow Raven... fell under the spell of a great barbed blade that nearly made him kill a friend... had a brief liaison with a Bengala, a woman who could transform into a snow-white tigress with a star on her forehead...

If even half the legends are reliable, Conan and his savage sword had some strange employers. One of the oddest was an alchemist named Gaspard, who hired him to steal a balm made from man-crushing vines of Khitai—the final ingredient of his plan to turn base metal into gold. But when Gaspard's treachery led the barbarian to toss him to his own vicious watchdogs, Conan failed to notice that the liquid mess on the floor had turned to gold.

In another tale, he hired on with an untrained army in a region rebelling against a Zamorian under-king. Unfortunately, he wound up on the losing side. He was hauled before King Fhal, who noted his resemblance to icons of a minor war god called Shan. The two made a bargain in which Conan would impersonate the deity. The real Shan was not amused—and attacked Conan, who defeated him. Surely this was some lesser demon, and not a god. Still, when Shan's former devotees knelt before Conan, he scorned the notion of being worshipped and rode away.

FIGHTING FOR ALMURIC

What is known for certain about this period is that at one point he joined the army of Almuric, yet another rebellious prince of Koth. Almuric's mad and motley horde "swept through the lands of Shem like a devastating sandstorm and drenched the outlands of Stygia with blood." The mercenaries then sliced their way through to the black kingdoms, only to be annihilated on the fringe of the southern desert by a combination of Stygians and Kushites. Almuric himself died with 40 Stygian arrows in him—if anyone truly stopped fighting long enough to count.

Conan later thought of Almuric's army as a "great torrent, dwindling gradually as it rushed southward, to run dry at last in the sands of the naked desert." And, in the words of the Nemedian Chronicles: "The bones of its members—mercenaries, outcasts, broken men, outlaws—lay strewn from the Kothic uplands to the dunes of the wilderness."

DRUMS OF TOMBALKU

Not long afterward, Conan joined the mercenary army that the Zingaran Prince Zapayo da Kova raised on behalf of Argos. Koth was to invade Stygia from the north, and da Kova's band by sea from the south. At the last moment, however, King Strabonus decided a back-stabbing bargain was preferable to war and made his peace with Luxur. This left the mercenaries trapped in the Stygian desert—a geography with which Conan was becoming depressingly familiar by then...

Xuthal of the Dusk

Conan and the Brythunian slave girl Natala first came upon the mysterious lost city while seeking shelter from the harsh extremes of the Southern Desert. They immediately detected its weirdness when they found a yellow-skinned man lying near the gate as if dead. Dressed in silken tunic, his short sword sheathed in a cloth-of-gold scabbard at his side, he was cold to the touch—no wound upon him—yet he was untouched by decay. Confused and somewhat disquieted by the sight, they decided to enter the city anyway.

But they had only just passed by when the man arose and rushed at them—now alive and brandishing his sword—forcing Conan to sever his spine and toss the carcass down a well.

> BUT, IT'S NEARLY SUNSET—AND, WHILE THE SHADE FROM THE CITY MAY BE WELCOME NOW—

> IT'LL KEEP US EQUALLY FROM THE COLD OF THE DESERT NIGHT.

THALIS

The beautiful, dark-haired woman who confronted Conan and Natala in the desert city of Xuthal identified herself as Thalis, daughter of a Stygian king from the capital city of Luxur. She claimed to have been initiated into the sensual mysteries of the dusky goddess Derketo by age 15 before being abducted by a rebel prince, who perished in the desert. His camel had carried her to Xuthal. Thalis, sick of dreamers who slept half their lives away, wanted Conan to be her lover, but he spurned her, in favor of Natala. Thalis, however, would brook no refusal. She distracted Conan and dragged the Brythunian into a secret stone passage where she strung her up by her wrists, intending to sacrifice her to the city's god. While flaying Natala with a jewel-handled whip of seven silk cords, Thalis did not spy the great black shapeless mass which loomed up behind her... until she was pulled into it, like a leaf into a whirlwind. And thus perished Thalis the Stygian.

"A City of the Mad"

In the saga of Conan the Cimmerian, the city of Xuthal is virtually a character in its own right. Conan himself called it "a city of the mad," filled with "damned degenerates," while the Stygian woman Thalis claimed the city was "actually one great palace."

TO DREAM, PERCHANCE TO DIE...

Within the city, they found fresh food and liquor set out, as if for a feast, and people rising at twilight to walk about as if in a trance. From the mysterious Stygian woman Thalis, they learned that Xuthal's inhabitants lived most of their lives in a dreamlike state induced by the juice of the fabled black lotus. During the day, they slept, showing not the slightest sign of sentient life. But according to her, they were filled with "exotic ecstasies, beyond the ken of ordinary men." Even so, the dream-walkers united to attack the barbarian "desecrator."

He and Natala managed to survive the night but left town with the next dawn, when its denizens resumed their death-sleep.

The open desert was a harsh environment, but it was better than the madness of Xuthal—and at least now they had plenty of wine and water!

AND THE SUN BEATS DOWN...

On foot with supplies running low in the midst of the vast tracts of the southern desert, Conan and Natala had little choice but to seek shelter in the lost city.

THOG

Thog was the god of Xuthal, a darkness that light would not dissipate. Its ever-changing, toadlike features were, according to the Chronicles, "as dim and unstable as those of a specter seen in a mirror of nightmare." It was a solid thing, the very outline of which changed subtly even as one looked at it.

When it reached out a dark tentacle to touch Natala's naked flesh, still dangling from the wrists thanks to Thalis, the girl knew such fear and shame as she had never dreamed of. And in that instant, she also knew, whatever form of life Thog might be, it was not a mere beast!

FAREWELL TO XUTHAL

Conan feared the supernatural, yet the sight of Natala in Thog's inhuman grip filled him with murderous fury—and he attacked. Tentacles pulled him into its mouth, where its hot breath poisoned him. Tearing free, he ripped at the thing with his blade. When he managed to blind the thing, it toppled into a great round well from which no sound echoed back.

As he and Natala departed, she groused that he had caused their troubles by looking so admiringly at Natala.

Conan snorted: "When the oceans drown the world, women will still take time for jealousy. Did I tell the Stygian to fall in love with me? After all, she was only human!"

"COSMIC LUST"
When Thog glared at the helpless Natala, she shook at the "cosmic lust" reflected in those great pools of light that could have been eyes.

REQUIEM FOR A GOD
Glistening with sweat and blood, Conan shrugged off his wounds, saying, "Well, you can't fight a devil out of Hell and come off with a whole skin!"

NATALA

She was a Brythunian, who had been carried off into slavery—and then got lucky. Seeing her in the slave market of a city in Shem that Prince Almuric's army had stormed, Conan impulsively purchased her. Since this is the only time in the Chronicles when the Cimmerian is known to have owned a slave, it's presumed that either he found her blonde beauty bewitching or he pitied her—likely both. She was grateful, since it was a vast improvement over a fate as a Shemitish seraglio. After Almuric's force was butchered by Stygians and Kushites, the two fled across the burning desert. When their camel died, they continued on foot. Natala was touched when she was given the last of their water to drink, not knowing that Conan was grimly considering ending her life with a merciful swordstroke—when he spotted the lost city of Xuthal not far off...

CONAN

SCOURGE OF THE SEAS

Mention the name "Conan the Cimmerian" to either Hyborian Age scholar or neophyte reader and the image usually conjured up is that of a bronzed, battle-axe-wielding barbarian. Yet one role he assumed several times in both canon and fable was that of a pirate.

CONAN THE BARACHAN

After his wanderings to Xuthal and Tombalku, he made his way to the Western Ocean, where he was picked up by Barachan pirates, a loose-knit assemblage based off the coast of Zingara. Most of the so-called "Barachans" were actually Argosseans, who carried on their nation's sea-based rivalry with Zingara outside the law. Strangely, although Conan remained with the Barachans for some time, little is certain concerning his exploits among them, except the manner of his leaving them! But when did pirates ever take the time to keep a record of their plundering?

As ever, legend leaps in where the Nemedian Chronicles do not deign to tread. After an adventure or three, Conan is said to have assumed command of a vessel known as the *Hawk,* which was then sunk by pirates from Khitai. Later yarns have Conan sailing with them to the far-off east, where he became embroiled in a deadly power struggle between the Stygian sorcerer Thoth-amon and a powerful pre-Cataclysmic mage. Supposedly, he was magically transported back west and dumped into the waters near Port Tortage. But some feel the scribe who recorded this cycle of legends was unduly influenced by the fumes of the black lotus when he committed it to parchment.

DOWN WITH THE SEA AND SHIPS

Other tales tell of the Cimmerian serving briefly on the *Red Hand* under Strombanni the Messantian, a Barachan pirate mentioned in the Chronicles. Strombanni was already seeking the fabled Treasure

of Tranicos, as was his rival, the Zingaran buccaneer Black Zarono. As for Captain Conan, he seems to have had trouble keeping a ship under his sea legs. One, called the *Cockatoo*, is mentioned only because it was sunk by Zingarans. Eventually, his stint with the Barachan pirates came to an end. The Nemedian Chronicles relate that, having made even more enemies than friends, he had to slip out of a tight spot in Port Tortage by making a foredoomed attempt to row—and then swim—the Western Ocean!

FROM BARACHAN TO BUCCANEER TO BARBARIAN

Fortunately, before his arms gave out—and this, too, is vouchsafed by the Chronicles—he encountered the *Wastrel*, a freebooter. Events took their normal course, and Conan was soon in command of another pirate galley, this one Zingaran, not Barachan. In the eyes of some Hyborians, there was a fundamental difference between these two branches of the Red Brotherhood: the Barachans were outlaws pure and simple, while Zingaran buccaneers often acted under a loose commission from that kingdom's ruler, which mostly just encouraged them to plunder ships that flew any but the Zingaran flag.

A Cimmerian, Conan was reputedly more eager to prey on Zingaran shipping than most buccaneers were. Eventually, certain Zingaran ships brought him down off the coasts of Shem, and he was forced to escape inland. From this point forward, he again became a land-roving adventurer. But he left behind a bloody, sea-salted trail that would fill many a sea chanty for eons to come.

ISLES OFF THE COAST

BARACHAN ISLES

Also known as the Barachas, or simply Baracha, this archipelago in the Western Ocean lay some distance from the Zingaran coast. Baracha was the stronghold of bloodthirsty pirates who preyed on the shipping of every nation, but especially that of Zingara,

Woe betide the pirate who fell into Zingaran hands, for more than one ship's crew was executed in Kordava. Legend has it that even Conan was once captured after his own Barachan vessel was sunk. He was held briefly in Zingara's Coast Prison No. 4, better known as "Torture Rock." And it is also said that he had a particular enemy among the Barachans, a pirate captain named Bor'aqh Sharaq.

CHIVALRY ASHORE...

"Zingara with its chivalry." Such is the reputation of Zingara according to the Nemedian Chronicles. But despite that reputation, Zingaran sailors seem to have often been employed as buccaneers.

...PIRACY ASEA

Argossean freebooters based in the Barachan Isles competed with Zingaran pirates for booty. Strange, then, that a certain Cimmerian would come to lead forces from both sides on separate occasions.

"...Zingara with it's Chivalry..."

HEAVE TO IT, MY HEARTIES!

AYE, CONAN.

ZINGARA

It was a land ruled by minor princes, who paid mere lip service to the crown at Kordava. Its seamen were often pirates and its proud mounted warriors seemed always to be engaged in bloody civil wars.

Its people were the mixed descendants of the inhabitants of the age-old Valley of Zingg, Hyborian tribesmen, and Pictish invaders who crossed the Black and Thunder rivers. Since some believe the ancient valley dwellers to be of Shemitish origin, it is disputed whether or not Zingara is to be considered a "non-Hyborian" kingdom.

Numerous rivers flowed through Zingara, including the Alimane, which also formed Zingara's border with Poitain, one of Aquilonia's most powerful provinces. Aside from Kordava and one or two other great cities, it was a kingdom mostly of mountains, woods, and fields where farmers prayed to Mitra for rain.

Precisely how the love of the sea entered the Zingarans' veins cannot be known, but in Conan's time, that nation was engaged in a heated rivalry with neighboring Argos for trade supremacy. Each strove to build and maintain the largest merchant fleet in that part of the world. Yet it was the king of Zingara, not Argos, who gave semi-official status to buccaneers, or freebooters, by making them agents of the crown. The leadership of

URBAN DIVERSIONS

Given Zingara's ghoul-infested forests and "fiend-haunted swamps" it's no wonder that wealthy Zingarans—or perhaps the occasional Cimmerian with coin—flocked to the cities.

YES, THE WAR IS OVER, AND YET THE SPECTRE OF WARS PASSING STILL HAUNTS THE STREETS. ONCE-PROUD FARMERS, THEIR CROPS DESTROYED, HAVE SLOGGED IN FROM THE COUNTRY-SIDE TO BEG CROSS-LEGGED AT THE CURBS. JUST BEYOND THE PALE GLOW OF TAVERNS' LIGHTS ARE THE VACANT-EYED STARES OF MEN GROWN GAUNT WITH HUNGER AND DEFEAT.

Argos was more prone to calling all such agents pirates—although no doubt there were many Argosseans who cheered wildly when they beheld a Zingaran galley sinking far out at sea, her prow and sails set aflame by a torch made in Messantia!

PIRATES WILL BE PIRATES

When not preying on Zingaran shipping, Conan and the Barachan pirates often followed their noses to ports, where grog and women awaited.

CONAN

SOUTH OF STYGIA

After such a long spell at sea, the Cimmerian was ready for a place where the surface he stood on did not pitch and sway with each rising and falling of the waves, and where his world was not limited by the distance from prow to stern. There were reports that, while heading eastward through Ophir, he became embroiled in a dispute between two military units: the Black Cloaks and the Iron Maidens, a band of armored women. But his ultimate destination would be the lands south of serpent-haunted Stygia. Hearing that wars were in the offing along the Stygian border (and when were they not?), Conan joined another armed force—one that bore a familiar name.

THE FREE COMPANIONS

In Conan's day, "The Free Companions" was apparently a common designation for mercenary companies. Once—was it really a decade earlier?—Conan had fought for a group that went by the same name. With them, he had raided the borders of Koth, Zamora, and Turan. After signing on with the new Free Companions, he was dispatched to the post at Sukhmet, which guarded the frontier between Stygia and Darfar. There, he served under a man named Zarallo, but he soon grew weary of the inactive life. When a female soldier of fortune called Valeria left the camp for the mysterious kingdoms far to the south of Stygia, Conan followed her—with more on his mind than a bit of fresh air. That pursuit led them to the time-lost city called Xuchotl.

TWO FOR THE ROAMING

Only legend fills in the details of what happened after Conan and Valeria left Xuchotl. One cycle of tales has them caught up in yet another blood feud, this one involving two native tribes, a gigantic, intelligent Golden Serpent, and a "god" known as the Living Wind. By this time, they'd seen enough of the jungle, so they headed north to renew lives of piracy. It is doubtful, however, that the two of them would ever have been able to agree on which was to be captain. At some point, Conan and Valeria went their separate ways, and there is no record in the Nemedian Chronicles of their ever meeting again.

ALWAYS TIME FOR A TREASURE HUNT

Alone again, Conan's next stop was Keshan. Somewhere in that kingdom was ancient city of Alkmeenon, in whose lost ruins lay the priceless treasure known as the Teeth of Gwahlur. In order to remain in Keshan while secretly searching for these jewels, he volunteered to train its armies and lead them against their hereditary enemy, the neighboring kingdom of Punt. Border skirmishes gave him ample opportunity to prove his fighting and leadership prowess. In the end, he headed north out of Keshan—without the jewels, but, naturally, with a woman.

East and South of Kush

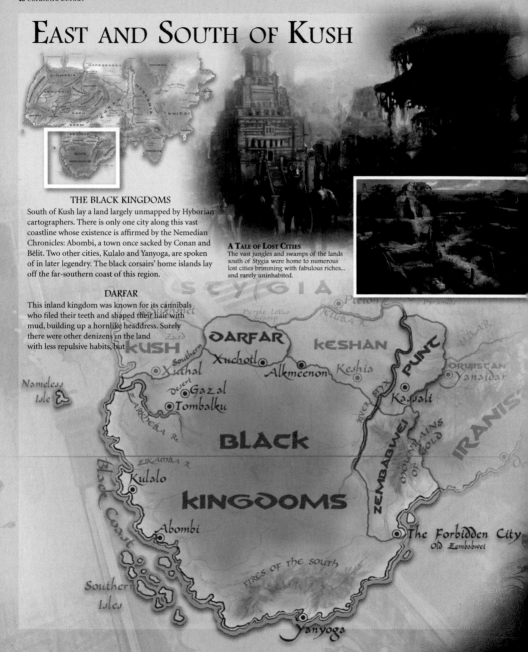

THE BLACK KINGDOMS

South of Kush lay a land largely unmapped by Hyborian cartographers. There is only one city along this vast coastline whose existence is affirmed by the Nemedian Chronicles: Abombi, a town once sacked by Conan and Bêlit. Two other cities, Kulalo and Yanyoga, are spoken of in later legendry. The black corsairs' home islands lay off the far-southern coast of this region.

A Tale of Lost Cities
The vast jungles and swamps of the lands south of Stygia were home to numerous lost cities brimming with fabulous riches... and rarely uninhabited.

DARFAR

This inland kingdom was known for its cannibals who filed their teeth and shaped their hair with mud, building up a hornlike headdress. Surely there were other denizens in the land with less repulsive habits, but

sharp-fanged Darfars
often retained their
sweet tooth for "long pig" even
after they had been carried off by
slavers from Shem.

PUNT

Bordered partly by the River Styx,
Punt was blessed with an abundance of precious
metals found in its portion of the river. Its people
worshipped an ivory goddess. Like the other black
kingdoms, Punt was often subjected to raids by
slavers from Stygia and Shem.

ZEMBABWEI

Zembabwei was perhaps the most powerful of these
southernmost kingdoms, and was said to be ruled by
"twin kings." Virtually nothing is known of this rising
empire in the south, although some legends say its
people worshipped the Stygian serpent-god Set under
the alternate name Damballah.

UNKNOWN SOUTH
Even the Nemedian
Chronicles describe
this sprawling region
sparsely, saying that
they were "the vast
black kingdoms of the
Amazons, the
Kushites, the Atlaians,
and the hybrid empire of
Zembabwei."

CONAN

OF THE BORDER

Conan soon joined the armed forces of Aquilonia as a scout along its border with the Pictish Wilderness. Although only that vast tract of swamp and forest lay between the mightiest kingdom of the age and the Western Ocean, and although land-locked Aquilonia surely desired a seaport, that savage race remained unconquered. Indeed, in the centuries to come, it was the Picts who were destined one day to overrun the Hyborian kingdoms, not the other way around!

THROUGH A MIRROR DARKLY

With his keen intelligence, Conan must have recognized the similarities between the situations facing the Pictish Wilderness and Cimmeria, both of which were targets of imperial Aquilonia. While few records were kept of battles between civilized troops and savages in the Pictish Wilderness, legends abound of Conan's exploits there. The Nemedian Chronicles aver that the Pictish menace was increasing in size and ferocity. Fort Tuscelan offered the only protection for the Aquilonian settlers of the region known as Conajohara, which lay between the Black River and Thunder River. Despite Conan's valiant efforts, the fort was destroyed by the dusky-skinned horde. In the aftermath of that slaughter, a border man phrased it best: "Barbarism is the natural state of mankind. Civilization is unnatural. It is a whim of circumstance. And barbarism must always inevitably triumph."

LEGEND OF A HERO

Events after the fall of Fort Tuscelan are very much in dispute among scholars of the Hyborian Age. One prominent legend says that Conan's heroism in attempting to warn the fortress of impending doom led to his being promoted to captain. It goes on to describe how he led the

Aquilonians to ultimate victory at a place called Massacre Meadow, where he saved a second fort, called Velitrium. For that, he was promoted to general and summoned back to Tarantia for a triumphal parade. He left the western frontier, expecting to return soon.

POLITICS AND PIRACY

According to these sources, Conan had his triumph in Aquilonia's capital. But, having aroused the envy of King Numedides, he was plied with drugged wine and chained in the Iron Tower. Yet he had friends as well as enemies in Tarantia, and he was spirited out of prison. Riding back to the frontier, he found his Bossonian troops scattered and learned that there was a price on his head. So he swam Thunder River and struck out across the dank forests of Pictland toward the distant sea.

The Chronicles pick up the tale from there, placing the Cimmerian alone in the Pictish Wilderness, where he got involved in a four-way tug-of-war over the lost treasure of the legendary pirate Tranicos. One competitor was killed by a demon, the other two by Picts, and Conan sailed away with the late nobleman's niece and her ward.

There is a variant tradition that says Conan sailed away on a ship bearing several Aquilonians, who had come north to persuade him to join their bid to overthrow King Numedides. Either way, the fact remains that the next time the Chronicles speak of Conan, he has become king of Aquilonia.

ZOGAR SAG

In his younger days, this Pictish wizard stole an ale-carrying mule pack that belonged to a wealthy Velitrium merchant named Tiberias. Found drunk, Zogar Sag was jailed, but he escaped, vowing revenge. Soon afterward, Tiberias seemingly went mad and rode out of the fort with a glassy stare. His corpse was later found by Conan and Balthus. But Zogar Sag's thirst for revenge was not slaked, and he caused his fellow Picts to launch a savage revolt against Aquilonian incursions in the Wilderness.

THE MAGIC AND THE MYSTERY

According to the forest demon, Zogar Sag was his brother—a child birthed by a woman from Gwawela who had slept in a grove sacred to the ancient god Jhebbal Sag. The wizard's magic united the Picts into into a force at least fifteen clans strong, bent on retaking Conajohara from the hated Aquilonians. He summoned both the sabertooth and the great fanged python from the wilds—and brought the terrifying forest demon, as well.

DEATH OF A WIZARD

The tale of Zogar Sag's death, as related to Conan back at Velitrium, was passing strange. Apparently, during the final battle at Fort Tuscelan, the shaman was dancing unhurt amid the slain when he suddenly screamed and fell into the fire. No weapon had touched him, yet the teller swore there were red marks on his leg and belly, and his head had been almost severed from his body. His death took the heart out of the Picts... and they fled.

MASTER OF MEN AND BEASTS
Whirling about in garments formed of feathers, Zogar Sag wielded an almost hypnotic power over the Picts and the beasts of the forest.

BALTHUS KNOWS WITHOUT ASKING THAT IT IS ZOGAR SAG.

THE FOREST DEMON

No non-Pict knew what it looked like, this demon that did the bidding of Zogar Sag. Yet the thing killed Aquilonians by luring them to their deaths. While leading the settlers toward the safety of Velitrium, Conan heard a voice calling to him from a nearby grove, where he found a weird, green witch-fire that shimmered with purpose. Out of the fire rose a taloned demon that looked like some huge predatory bird. But Conan had learned over the years that any being clothed in material flesh could be slain by material weapons. So he brought it down with his slicing sword that cut crimson wounds on its legs and belly... and nearly severed its head. Only when he heard how Zogar Sag had died miles away, did Conan sense the truth of the connection between shaman and demon.

SAGAYETHA

The shaman is dead—long live the shaman! In legends that fill the gaps between Conajohara's fall and the death of Zogar Sag, there are tales of the shaman Sagayetha. He was the nephew of Zogar Sag and when his uncle was killed, he became the Picts' new wizard.

WHAT WAS SHALL BE AGAIN

Once, long ago, when beasts and men spoke one language, all living things worshipped Jhebbal Sag. By Conan's time, most men had forgotten him... as had most of the animals. But those men and animals who did remember were brothers and spoke the same tongue. These were the men and beasts that Zogar Sag and his nephew Sagayetha, both of whom might have been descendants of the god, could command.

Among them were the deadly vipers that Sagayetha sent against the frontier soldiers. He also worked in concert with an Aquilonian traitor to destroy Velitrium. After dealing with the betrayer, Conan—now a captain—stole into the Picts' camp and beheaded Sagayetha. Seeing the shaman's head on a pike as the Cimmerian galloped toward them on Massacre Meadow, the Picts scattered—and Conan was soon promoted to general.

THE SIGN OF JHEBBAL SAG

Conan first saw the sign of Jhebbal Sag in a cave in the uninhabited mountains beyond the Vilayet Sea. Some time later, he had watched as a witch-finder of Kush scratched it in the sand on the banks of a nameless river. The man had told him it was sacred to Jhebbal Sag and to the creatures that still worshipped it. While on the way back to Fort Tuscelan, Conan carved the image in the dirt with his sword, then he and Balthus watched from hiding as a black panther slinked from the jungle, studied the sign—and fled as if in sudden panic. From that time forward, Conan told Balthus, they had no more to fear from beasts of Pict.

LIKE UNCLE, LIKE NEPHEW?

If Conan thought his battles with oversized Pictish beasts died with Zogar Sag, he was in for a rude suprise when his nephew Sagayetha took power.

CONAN

THE LIBERATOR

In the days of revolt, Conan was hailed as "the Liberator." He said that when the tyrant King Numedides lay dead at his feet, he "tore the crown from his gory head and set it on my own." But he still had much to learn, saying later, "I had prepared myself to take the crown, not to hold it." Yet, take the crown he did.

A PIRATE COMES SOUTH

Once more, legend steps forward to shine a light where facts are shadowy. According to one tale, after the events surrounding the search for Tranicos' treasure, the Cimmerian came south by ship from Pictland to Argos, since Aquilonia itself was landlocked. He was accompanied by Count Trocero of Poitain, the nobleman general Prospero, Dexitheus, priest of Mitra, and the councilor Publius. If this legend is true, it is fitting that he arrived in Aquilonia still wearing pirate garb he had acquired in the north—for he meant to plunder the crown of Aquilonia.

A GATHERING OF EAGLES

According to this tradition, Conan returned to the Hyborian lands already determined to unseat Numedides. He and his allies soon had an army of more than 10,000 men, many of them veterans who had served with Conan in the Lion Regiment at Velitrium andMassacre Meadow during the Pictish wars. Naturally, King Milo of Argos was eager to see this multitude leave his soil. Why risk angering his more powerful fellow monarch to the north? And why give Conan the idea that being king of Argos might be enough?

SWORDS ACROSS THE ALIMANE

The legend cycle says that Numedides' "advisor" Thulandra Thuu used sorcery against Conan's forces as they marched toward Tarantia. In addition, the Cimmerian did not realize that he had a traitor in his midst, betraying his every move. Ambushed as they attempted to cross the Alimane River, his forces were scattered across the countryside. But the men regrouped, and with the aid of the strange satyr-folk who inhabited the hills of Poitain, the rebel army gained a victory over Aquilonian forces personally led by Thulandra Thuu. But the real test was yet to come, as the army moved toward the capital.

DEATH OF A MAD KING

At last, Conan faced Numedides in the palace royal. Thulandra Thuu vanished by magic, and Nemedides soon lay dead, despite Conan's attempt to show him mercy. The new king named Dexitheus his chancellor, in recognition of good advice and service rendered during the rebellion. Ere long, his old councilor Publius was besieging him with treasury accounts, petitions, and advocates' briefs. Conan saw that responsibilities, as well as power, came with the crown.

BARBARIANS AT THE GATE

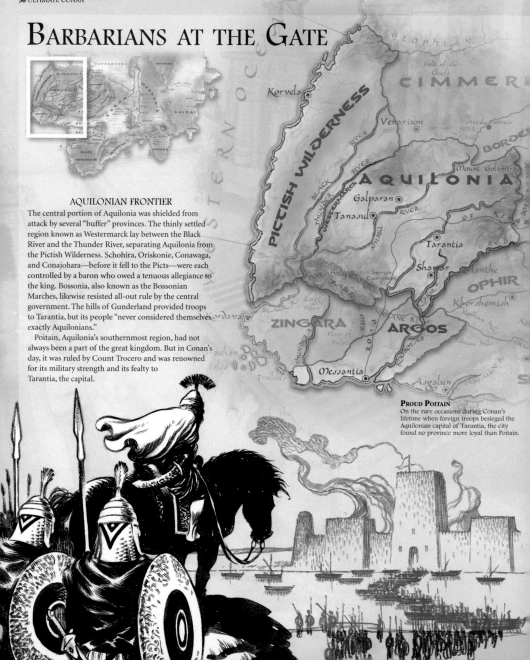

AQUILONIAN FRONTIER

The central portion of Aquilonia was shielded from attack by several "buffer" provinces. The thinly settled region known as Westermarck lay between the Black River and the Thunder River, separating Aquilonia from the Pictish Wilderness. Schohira, Oriskonie, Conawaga, and Conajohara—before it fell to the Picts—were each controlled by a baron who owed a tenuous allegiance to the king. Bossonia, also known as the Bossonian Marches, likewise resisted all-out rule by the central government. The hills of Gunderland provided troops to Tarantia, but its people "never considered themselves exactly Aquilonians."

Poitain, Aquilonia's southernmost region, had not always been a part of the great kingdom. But in Conan's day, it was ruled by Count Trocero and was renowned for its military strength and its fealty to Tarantia, the capital.

PROUD POITAIN
On the rare occasions during Conan's lifetime when foreign troops besieged the Aquilonian capital of Tarantia, the city found no province more loyal than Poitain.

KING NUMEDIDES

Numedides is little more than a name in the Nemedian Chronicles, a despot who lost his life and his crown to Conan. But legend has fleshed Numedides out—literally.

NUMEDIDES THE GOD

In these perhaps-apocryphal tales, he was a weak-minded tyrant who, having fallen under the thumb of the wizard Thulandra Thuu, took to bathing in the blood of virgins, holding conversations with trees and flowers, and ordering the golden coinage in his treasury recast into statues of himself. He became convinced that he was a deity who lacked only immortality. Woe to a kingdom, when madness wears the crown!

DELUSIONS OF ADEQUACY

Although teetering on the brink of madness, he began to recognize the depth of his self-delusion when he tried to molest the woman Alcina, who served Thulandra Thuu. The wizard ordered him to stop his advances, whereupon the king threatened to blast him with lightning. He then attacked the mage with the Sword of State—only to have his weapon parried with a mere wooden staff and sent flying back at him, slicing his ear. After the incident, he persisted in his attempts to order the wizard around, albeit more warily.

DEATH OF A DESPOT

And then—suddenly—Conan was there, backed by Dexitheus and a handful of soldiers. Deserted by Thulandra Thuu, Numedides begged for mercy, saying that Conan could not possibly kill an unarmed man. The Cimmerian would have been content merely to have him bound and gagged until they could find a madhouse for him. But when he tried to stab the barbarian from behind with a poisoned dagger, Conan saw that he would never be safe while Numedides was alive. So Conan strangled the king with his bare hands—and placed the crown upon his own head.

A LOOSE END

When Conan had burst into the throne room to face Numedides and his mage, Thulandra Thuu had fled, leaving his beautiful spy Alcina alone and cowering in fear. Facing the man that she had spied on, betrayed, and very nearly assassinated with poison, she knelt before him and blithely

lied that she had been "ensorcelled"—forced to do the wizard's bidding. Conan spared her life because she was a woman, but said that if she were ever again found in Aquilonia, she would lose her pretty head.

REDEMPTION

Alcina never actually left the realm. One day, not long afterward, she had her chance for revenge when Conan crawled out of a river, half drowned by the wizard's treachery. Gasping for air, he vowed to forget her betrayal if she helped him. She hesitated—then stabbed the Thulandra Thuu's Khitan servant before he could kill Conan. The king kept his word. After he beheaded Thulandra Thuu, he rewarded her richly.

ALCINA

The spy wore... very little. In the legend of Conan the Liberator, Alcina looms large. The Cimmerian rebel was intrigued by the dark-haired dancing girl he beheld in Messantia's Inn of the Nine Drawn Swords. Little did he know that she was a spy for the powerful and conniving sorcerer Thulandra Thuu, although not always the most effective sort. She did manage to poison General Amulius Procas for her master, but when she tried the same trick on Conan, she would have been wise to stick around long enough to make sure it worked. In the end, after several more twists and turns, Alcina proved herself useful to the Cimmerian, and he bestowed upon her a villa at Elymia. And she, in turn, was loyal to him from that day forth.

LIBERATOR OR USURPER?

Tradition holds that Numedides was a tyrant, but that claim relies mostly upon Conan's own words. One night, he spoke to Prospero of men maimed by Numedides' goons, of sons who died in his dungeons, of wives and daughters carried off into his seraglio. If true, no wonder Conan was hailed as a liberator when he struck for the throne.

CONAN

THE KING

As a pair of scholars once wrote, Conan soon learned that being ruler of a mighty kingdom like Aquilonia "was no bed of houris." His crown rested most uneasily on his black-maned head—and how could it not have done so? To many, he was not "the Liberator," but "the Usurper."

The first major threat to his reign came perhaps a year after he seized power, when plotters attempted to put a native-born king on the throne. Not long afterward, the kings of Ophir and Koth conspired to try to bring down Conan, and they even succeeded in capturing him. Both schemes were foiled as much by sorcerers—in fact, by a total of three sorcerers—as by the redoubtable Cimmerian's own efforts. Conan had always disliked wizardry, but over the years he had gradually lost most of his fear of it, and in his middle years he had few qualms about accepting magical help when it was offered.

THE HAUNTER OF THE RING

Legends sprouted up around Conan the king as profusely as ever they had about the barbarian, the pirate, or the soldier of fortune. For instance, soon after the first assassination plot was foiled—thanks in part to the inadvertent aid of Thoth-Amon—it's said that Conan's friend Trocero ran into some marital problems. He was tormented by the fact that his wife Evlena had tried to kill him—not that she recalled doing so. When Conan learned that a rejected suitor had given her a ring that had once belonged to Thoth, Conan finessed the ring onto the plotter's finger. When a demon came for Evlena, it carried him off instead.

A MATTER OF LINEAGE

About five years into his reign, Conan was unseated and imprisoned a second time, by a second group of plotters. He had left himself vulnerable to such schemes by never marrying or producing an heir during his half decade rule. Therefore his reign lacked a feeling of permanence, the sense that a dynasty was beginning. This time it took longer for Conan to re-establish his rule, but

he did so—once again with some timely help from sorcery. Having regained his throne, he announced that he would wed the young woman who had helped him escape.

At precisely this point, the Nemedian Chronicles break off, with the victorious barbarian king still standing among the blood of the battlefield. After Conan became king once more, there is not a single fact known for certain about his life—not even whether he actually carried out his marriage intentions, let alone whether said queen produced an heir to give legitimacy to his reign. There are only legends...

THE PERSISTENCE OF LEGEND

And yet, those tales exist in abundance: Legends of Conan's return to Nemedia to collect his bride-to-be... the wedding night... the abduction of his queen and his single-handed pursuit of her across half a world... his children, especially a firstborn son called Conn... the deaths of some of his greatest surviving enemies...

In short, these legends seem to show that Conan's life as king was no less eventful than his rise to kingship had been.

"AH, THE PROUD, VAIN *REBEL FOUR:*

"*DION*, WHO THINKS THE CROWN OF AQUILONIA WILL BE *HIS* WHEN THE BARBARIAN USURPER IS CAST DOWN...

"*GROMEL*, WHO DESIRES TO COMMAND THE PRESTIGIOUS *BLACK DRAGON* REGIMENT...

"DWARFISH *VOLMANA* WHO SEEKS POWER AND POSITION

"OF THE REBEL FOUR, ONLY THE POET *RINALDO* HAS NO *PERSONAL* AMBITION.

"THE FOUR OF THEM AND I HAVE *PLOTTED WELL,* THESE PAST WEEKS.

FOR MADE BOLD BY *LIQUOR* I'VE SMUGGLED OVER THE BORDER, THE HEATHEN *PICTS* ASSAIL THE *WESTERN BOUNDARIES* OF THESE *HYBORIAN LANDS...*

AND IT WAS EASY FOR *VOLMANA* TO PERSUADE *KING NUMA* OF NEMEDIA TO REQUEST *AID* FROM AQUILONIA TO *SMASH* THEM.

BOTH *COUNT TROCERO* AND *PROSPERO*, KING CONAN'S RIGHT-HAND MAN, HAVE ALREADY *LEFT* FOR THE FRONTIER...

financed much of the plot, planned to take the throne on Conan's death—but the Count of Thune intended that he, too, would soon die. Ironically, it was Dion who brought the whole scheme crashing down. Through his folly, Thoth-amon reclaimed possession of his pilfered magic ring. With Dion dead at his feet, he unleashed an unholy terror upon nighted Tarantia.

VOLMANA

Through his princely kin in Nemedia, the dwarfish Count of Karaban persuaded King Numa of the neighboring kingdom to summon Count Trocero. This meant that Prospero and an imperial escort would go with him, leaving only Conan's personal bodyguard and the Black Legion in the city.

GROMEL

The towering, Bossonian-born commander of the Black Legion despised Pallantides, leader of the Black Dragons, the king's elite guard. Gromel desired to unite both forces under his own command, and if his monarch were to be slaughtered along the way... so be it. Through him, Ascalante bribed an officer of the king's guard to lead his men away from the sovereign's door at midnight.

RINALDO

Of the plotters, the poet alone had no personal ambition, but he despised this barbarian usurper of a civilized throne. His song "The Lament for the King" idealized the late Numedides and denounced Conan as "that black-hearted savage from the abyss." Even the Cimmerian was touched by his poems, and rejected Prospero's suggestion that he be hanged. He felt that "a great poet is greater than any king," and that Rinaldo's rhymes would live forever.

ASCALANTE AND THE FOUR
Ascalante considered himself the puppetmaster of the plot to assassinate King Conan, but Dion, Volmana, Gromel, and Rinaldo—the so-called "Rebel Four"—considered him their dupe.

YOU NEED NOT BE *NERVOUS,* MILORD, ASCALANTE'S PLOT *CANNOT FAIL.*

ASCALANTE CAN MAKE *MISTAKES* THE SAME AS *ANY* MAN.

NOT *HE*--ELSE I HAD BEEN NOT HIS *SLAVE,* BUT HIS *MASTER.*

EH--?

AN ENEMY OF AN ENEMY IS HARDLY A FRIEND
When Dion, Baron of Attalus, showed Ascalante's slave a ring he had bought from a Shemitish thief, who claimed to have stolen it from a wizard, little did he know with whom he was dealing...

THE PLOTTERS

In the first year of King Conan's reign, five men plotted to bring down this barbarian usurper—and they very nearly succeeded.

COUNT ASCALANTE

Exiled for earlier sins, Ascalante, Count of Thune, had resigned himself to raiding caravans for the rest of his life. But when four plotters and smuggled him back into the kingdom, old ambitions stirred. He snuck liquor over the border into Pictland, hoping that the savages would draw troops out of Tarantia. Then the stage would be set for the city to fall to him once he and 16 "desperate rogues" killed Conan. And it might have worked, but for his sullen, dusky slave... the somber, gaunt giant called Thoth-amon.

DION

Perhaps Ascalante was right in saying that Conan should have executed all men who retained a trace of royal blood—such as Dion, the fat baron of Attalus. Dion, who

THE DEMON OF THE RING

Thoth-amon cared nothing about Aquilonia or its kings, whether blue-blooded or barbarian born. He wanted only to reclaim the freedom he had lost when Ascalante gained possession of his stolen magic ring—and revenge on Ascalante for enslaving him!

When once more the ring was in his hands, the Stygian wizard summoned a huge, baboon-like demon. He tossed to it a sandal belonging to Ascalante and commanded him to kill the one who wore it... as well as everyone with him! With that last impulsive outburst, Thoth-amon sent doom out to the other plotters and to the Cimmerian, as well.

"WHO DIES FIRST?"

When the plotters sprung their trap at midnight, they did not catch Conan sleeping, as they had hoped. Rather, they found their usurper-king armored, axe-in-hand. Conan proceeded to wreak havoc among the 20 men who attacked him. He killed all within his immediate reach—even Rinaldo, whom for an instant he tried to spare.

...TO MEET THE FAST-APPROACHING HORROR WITH AN ARC OF HIS GLEAMING AXE--

As his attackers advanced, the Cimmerian, though severely wounded, growled: "Who dies first?"

Ascalante, last survivor of the plotters, was desperately rushing at Conan, knife raised, when there was a rushing of air—and the demon arrived, slashing and slaying. The Count died of fear before it could touch him. But Conan, roused to fury rather than to fear, slew the demon, retained the throne, and called for a drink.

BE HE MAN OR BEAST...
Undaunted by the demon's fearful appearance—which was so horrible that not even Thoth-amon could bear to look at it—Conan went to work with his axe.

"AYE—AND ALL WITH HIM!"
Having summoned the demon with the power of his ring, Thoth-amon baited the demon with a sandal, saying: "Find him who wore it, and destroy him! Kill him! Aye—and all with him!"

THEN, A TENUOUS SHADOW HOVERS-- GROWING IN SIZE AND CLARITY, TILL IT SOUNDS OUT DISTINCT AND HORRIFIC.

IT'S OUTLINE IS NOT UNLIKE A GIGANTIC BABOON-- BUT NO SUCH APE EVER WALKED THE EARTH, NOT EVEN IN MONSTER-BIRTHING STYGIA.

YOU HAVE CHOSEN WELL, O GOD OF SERPENTS TO SEND ME SUCH A SERVITOR!

ACKNOWLEDGMENTS

Roy Thomas would like to thank the following people who were of importance to this book:

Kurt Busiek for suggesting that DK have me write it... Fredrik Malmberg, Thommy Wojciechowski, and Joakim Zetterberg of Paradox Entertainment/Conan Properties for their diligence in coming up with good copies of much of the artwork... Brian Saliba at DK Publishing for his excellent efforts in editing pieces and patches of information into coherent form... Also at DK: Carl Raymond, Dirk Kaufman, Mark Johnson Davies, and Bess Braswell... Todd McFarlane for his kind words in his foreword... my late friend Jim Neal for the Conan Comics Chronology he gifted me with many years ago... Marvel editor Stan Lee, Marvel publisher Martin Goodman, and Glenn Lord, longtime literary agent for the REH estate, for between them making it possible for me to spend so many happy years lost in the Hyborian Age... and, most of all, to Robert E. Howard, who in the 1930s created as wonderful a fantasy world as any present-day gamer could ever dream of. Know, O Prince... that REH was the greatest!

Conan Properties would like to thank all Conan artists, who with their different portrayals of the Cimmerian, show that he is so much more than a one-man war machine: among others, Frank Frazetta, Gary Gianni, Ken Kelly, Gregory Manchess, Cary Nord, Alex Ross, P. Craig Russell, Mark Schultz, and Tim Truman. Among the artists from the Marvel era: John Buscema, Gil Kane, Barry Windsor-Smith, and others. We also want to thank a few other barbarians who helped make this book possible: Scott Allie and the Conan crew at Dark Horse Comics, Judy Hansen, Conan know-it-alls Rusty Burke, Jim Keegan, Patrice Louinet, and Paul Sammon. Thanks to Steve Gold, THQ, Nihilistic, Funcom, and Mongoose Publishing. Also to Larry Marder, Suzy Thomas, and Todd McFarlane at McFarlane Toys, Ginjer Buchanan and Susan Allison at Penguin Books, and Mike Degler at Brady Games. Thanks to Roy Thomas and Brian Saliba for writing, editing, and making this book happen!

Last, and most importantly, a great big thank you to every fan of Robert E. Howard and Conan. Because of you, Hyboria is alive and well, by Crom!

HITHER CAME THE
COMPLETE EDITION...

Get the rest of Conan's adventurous and bloody history in the full edition of *Conan: The Ultimate Guide*, written by Roy Thomas, world-renowned Conan comic author.

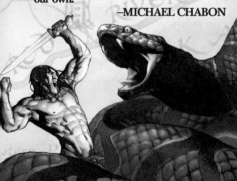

- Artwork from masters such as Frank Frazetta, John Buscema, and Cary Nord

- Original cover art by Alex Ross

- Foreword by Todd McFarlane

"Robert E. Howard dreamed Conan the Cimmerian for himself, and set him free to roam the world of his own Hyborian soul; but first in his years at Marvel Comics and now with this encyclopedia culmination, Roy Thomas dreamed him for all of us, and made that world come vividly to life within our own."

—MICHAEL CHABON

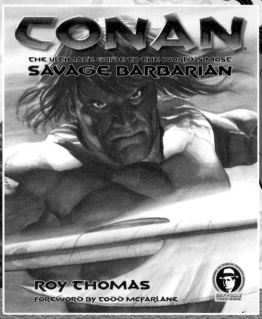

CONAN

THE ULTIMATE GUIDE TO THE WORLD'S MOST
SAVAGE BARBARIAN

ROY THOMAS
FOREWORD BY TODD MCFARLANE

DK
www.dk.com